FORSAKE ME NOT

FORSAKE ME NOT

Kay D. Rizzo

r2

REVIEW AND HERALD® PUBLISHING ASSOCIATION
HAGERSTOWN, MD 21740

Copyright © 1992 by Review and Herald® Publishing Association

The author assumes full responsibility for the accuracy of all facts and
quotations as cited in this book.

This book was edited by Mark Ford
Designed by Bill Kirstein
Cover illustration by Scott Snow
Typeset: 10.5/11.5 Century Light Condensed

PRINTED IN U.S.A.

97 96 95 94 93 92 10 9 8 7 6 5 4 3 2 1

Library of Congress Cataloging in Publication Data
Rizzo, Kay D., 1943-
    Forsake me not / Kay D. Rizzo.
        p.   cm.
    1. Daniels, Megan.   2. Feldman, Michael J.   3. Seventh-day Adventists—
United States—Biography.   4. Adventists—United States—Biography.
I. Title.
BX6191.R59   1992
286.7'092—dc20
[B]   91-40875
                                                                        CIP

ISBN 0-8280-0647-4

Dedicated

to my sister, Connie.
When it came to choosing sides,
you were always on mine.
Thanks.

Thanks also to

Dr. Carl Henning,
Ken Anderson,
and to the volunteers at the
Santa Cruz Suicide Intervention Hot Line.

Other books by Kay D. Rizzo

Determined to Love

Gospel in the Grocery Store

I Will Die Free

The Power of a Saint

Seasons of Discovery

Seasons of the Heart

Someone to Love Me

Up Against the Wall

When Love Returns

CHAPTER

1

Friday, at last! Megan Daniels smiled across the clutter on the desktops at Virgil Fitzsimmons, her coworker. The man's pencil-thin mustache eagerly turned up at the edges; a glimmer of hope flickered in his eyes. She recognized the look and busied herself with straightening her desk calendar and pencil holder. He'd misinterpreted her smile. Again.

Megan's golden brown hair and her intense gray eyes—eyes that could pierce through the toughest armor, male or female—had attracted attention and admiration since grade school. Her eyes—fire and ice! Friends said that her glance could melt your heart or freeze you in your place.

Slipping a stack of order forms inside a folder, Megan dropped it into the top drawer and pushed away from the desk. *I have two days of freedom*, she thought, *freedom from the confines of this claustrophobic office. Freedom from jangling telephones, screaming sales managers and rude customers! Best of all, I am free to spend two whole days with Alan.* A vision of wavy blond hair, laughing brown eyes and a perfect grin popped into her mind. *Mr. and Mrs. Alan Hendricks. Alan and Megan Hendricks. Mega—*

"Megan—" The shrill voice of Loretta, the office receptionist, broke through her daydream. "Megan, you have a call on line two."

Megan snapped alert and reached for the telephone. "This is Megan Daniels. How may I help you?"

"My," the caller replied, "don't you sound professional!"

Megan grinned, adopting her most engaging tone. "Why, how nice of you to call. Are you ready to invest in our advanced line of communication systems yet? You were considering the voice pager, I believe."

"Yeah," Herb Daniels replied. "Me and the longhorns could use one of your sophisticated beeper systems here on the ranch. I could sing the little dogies to sleep each night—just like in the old days."

"Personally, considering the distances you regularly encounter, I wouldn't recommend a voice-pager system. Besides they are fast becoming obsolete. Now the Alpha-Numeric system . . . " Her voice oozed with professionalism. "Perhaps our Executive Digital Sky Pager would serve your needs more fully. I could drop by your office this afternoon and present the advantages of the Executive system. And later, after we sign the contracts, I know a nice little out-of-the-way place we could catch a bite to eat."

Virgil's mouth dropped open at the mention of the top-of-the-line Executive Digital Sky Pager communications system. No salesperson in the Albuquerque branch had ever sold an Executive Digital Sky Pager. And when Megan suggested dining with the mysterious caller, his attention jammed into overdrive. Ever since Megan arrived at Western Communications as a sales representative, the vibrant young woman had repeatedly ignored all of the company salemen's advances up to and including the supervisor of sales. The thought that someone was actually getting through to her set Virgil's mind racing. Glancing over her desk Megan caught sight of Virgil's startled expression. She smiled mischievously.

"Megan! Enough! You win," her father conceded. "You can out palaver me anytime. Could you stop off at Garza's Feed Store on your way home and pick up an order I called in?"

Laughing, she twirled around in her chair and answered, "Sure, Dad. You're lucky you caught me before I left to pick up Alan." Virgil sank back into his chair, disappointed, yet relieved. He'd been set up. Again. He sighed and turned back to his desk.

"Hey," her father chuckled, "Alan's plane doesn't land for at least an hour, does it? The airport is only a 20 minute drive from your office, even in the worst Friday afternoon traffic."

"Be careful now," Megan retorted. "I seem to remember seeing you hyperventilate a time or two while you waited for Libby to make the trip from Tucumkari. Besides it's his first visit to the Daniels' Ranch and I want everything to go well."

After a long pause, Herb Daniels drawled, "Check! Won't hold you up any longer. Don't forget to stop at the feed store."

"You got it." Megan laughed and picked a piece of lint from her beige suit skirt. "Oh, by the way, did I get any mail?"

"Two bills from The Bon and a letter from New York City."

"Ah, Sara wrote." Megan's former roommate, Sara Panetta, was so faithful at keeping in touch.

"Ya' got one from the college library too."

"Probably a late charge for an overdue book or something. Thanks, Dad. See ya'." Megan dropped the phone back on the cradle.

In one smooth motion, Megan leaped to her feet, grabbed her brief-case and suit-jacket, then disappeared out of the door. Her no-nonsense, two-inch heels clicked on the brick red Mexican tile as she hurried down the arched hallway. The dry dusty heat of the pavement sprang up at her as she stepped out of the building. She shielded her eyes from the sun's bright glare.

Spending the time between her college graduation and her December wedding at home on the ranch with her dad had been a good idea. But to work so hard to graduate with high honors in order to sell beepers, of all things! Megan giggled to herself.

However, coming home hadn't been quite what she'd expected. Shortly after she arrived her father announced his intentions to marry the recently widowed Libby Strickland. Megan felt a twinge of pain at the thought. Of course she wanted her father to be happy. He'd been so lonely these past three years since her mom's death. He needed someone. Yet, watching a strange woman bustle about her mother's kitchen, sit in her mom's favorite rocker and slip a possessive arm about her dad's waist . . . *Maybe in time*, she thought. *Moving on—that's what Daddy called it.*

So easy to say, but so hard to do. Megan unlocked the car door of her faded red '73 Chevy. *If I didn't have Alan right now, I'd feel so alone. Thank You, Lord.*

She started the engine and groaned. "Great! The air conditioning is on the fritz again! How many times have I replaced those fuses? I need a new car." She banged the palm of her hand against the steering wheel. "Sorry, Beulah," she said affectionately, patting the cracked dashboard. "You're a fine old car, it's just sometimes I wish you were a little more comfortable. Yech!" She glanced down at the wrinkles in her skirt and grimaced.

Albuquerque's Friday afternoon traffic proved to be everything her father predicted. A scrungy pickup truck had tangled with a long-distance semi carrying farm produce from Texas. No one was hurt, fortunately, but the hundred or so melons strewn across all four lanes of traffic weren't doing so well. By the time she picked up her father's supplies and stopped off at the mall to buy some of Alan's favorite cheesecake, she felt like a Dallas Cowboy linebacker—after the big tackle. She pulled Beulah into the short-term parking area of the airport and dashed for the terminal.

"Of course," she mumbled, reading the schedule of incoming and outgoing flights, "Alan's plane would be on time and be landing at the farthest gate in the terminal. He's going to be frustrated with me for being late." She shot a rueful glance at her pumps and wished she'd brought along her running shoes. *Oh well,* she thought, *better get going.*

Halfway down the bustling terminal corridor she spotted Alan walking toward her. When he looked her way, she waved and broke into a run. She ignored the look of obvious irritation on his face and rushed into his arms.

"Hi, honey," she gasped. "You wouldn't believe the hassle I've had getting to the airport. On the freeway, a produce truck—"

Instead of returning her embrace, he clicked his tongue. "You're such a scatterbrain, Megan. When will you learn to plan ahead for these inconveniences? I have been waiting a good ten minutes for you."

"I'm sorry. You're right," Megan soothed. She knew from experience that if Alan fell into one of his moods the entire weekend could be ruined. She so wanted everything to go well. While her father had met him twice at the college, they'd never really had time to get acquainted. This would be the time. "So, how was your flight out from San Franscisco?"

The moment he opened his mouth to answer, Megan knew she'd asked the wrong question. His itemized list of complaints carried them all the way through the baggage-claim area and to her parked car. "Would you like to drive?" she offered.

Alan cast a jaundiced eye over the blushing Beulah. "The privilege is all yours, sweetheart." Inside the car, he attempted to make up for his cool reception in the terminal. "Guess I overreacted a bit back there," he apologized. "But you know how I hate being kept waiting."

"Hey, it's OK," Megan comforted. "I'm sorry, too. Let's just forget it and have a good time together."

During the 20 mile ride to the ranch, Alan appeared to relax. Coming up the driveway, he smiled when he first saw the two-story white wood-frame house she'd called home her entire life. "This place is like something out of a Zane Grey book, real down-home Americana.

All you need is a barking collie dog and a pinto pony standing at the fence."

As if on cue, Snapper, her collie dog and all-round best friend, bounded out from behind a rosebush at the side of the house. Megan glanced up at Alan and shrugged. "What can I say?" Less than a second later, the screen door flew open and Megan's dad appeared, followed by Libby. "Welcome to the Daniels' ranch, son." Herb reached for Alan's hand. "This here's my beautiful bride-to-be, Libby. And Libby, meet my soon-to-be son, Alan. Did Megan tell you how I always wanted a son to help me around the place?"

The sudden look of fright on Alan's face sent all three into fits of laughter. "Don't worry, Alan, you won't be expected to rope or brand a steer, at least not until after y'all get back from your honeymoon," Herb teased.

"Oh, Daddy!" Megan turned to Alan. "He is teasing, Alan—really," she assured him. "And he never stops."

"Aw, you'll get used to it." Herb threw his arm around Alan's shoulders and led him into the house. "Let me take you on up to your room so you can get settled before supper. Libby's famous chili and homemade johnnycake are ready for the takin'. Oh, Megan, I left your mail on the dining room table."

"Thanks, Dad," Megan called as the two most important men in her life disappeared up the stairs. She hurried to the dining room and began thumbing through her stack of letters. She could hear Libby working in the kitchen. "I hope you found everything you needed all right," Megan called. "And I hope you didn't go to too much trouble for us."

"No problem on either account," Libby assured her. "I enjoyed cooking up a family-sized batch of chili once again." Megan noticed the catch in Libby's voice. "I'd better check on the cornbread. Wouldn't want it to burn tonight of all nights."

It seemed strange to think that Libby might be a little nervous also. Megan smiled, then glanced at the two charge slips from The Bon. *Changing out of a schoolgirl's wardrobe into a professional woman's, sure is expensive*, she mused. Megan settled into a chair and opened the letter from Sara, her college roommate. Sara had majored in both Social Work and Music, and had done very well. Yet for all her brilliance at the keyboard, Sara's first love was people. So it surprised no one when, after graduation, she had landed an internship as a Social Worker with the New York City Welfare System.

"*Things are so different from campus life,*" the letter read. "*I am living with the greatest lady, Mama Grace, and her seven children, all foster kids. But you'd never know it by the way she loves them. And now, I guess I'm foster kid number eight. She's a genuine mother hen. The woman has her master's degree in Psychology and a Ph.D. in common sense.*"

Sara went on to tell about her work with the inner-city kids, and all the new friends she was making at the church. She was also a volunteer at the neighborhood community center. "*I was even a substitute teacher for grades 1-4 at the local church school for an entire week. Imagine me, the teacher's nightmare, teaching?*" Megan laughed at the picture of the boistrous Sara dealing with a roomful of equally energetic grade-schoolers.

The letter continued. "*Their regular teacher is due to have her first baby soon, but she's having a rough pregnancy. Mike Feldman, the youth pastor at our church, asked me if I knew of anyone who—if worst comes to worst—could finish out the school term. I almost laughed. I asked him, who, of all my friends, would be out of her mind enough to . . .* " Megan chuckled aloud. She could just see the poor pastor's reaction to Sara's irrepressible humor.

"What's so funny, Megan," Libby called from the kitchen. "Anything worth telling?"

Megan shook her head and grinned. "It would be impossible to explain. I'm afraid you'd have to know my old roommate, Sara, to understand."

Sara was the only person Megan had ever met who could maintain a stand-up comedy routine on the mishaps of campus life, flail her arms about like a baton twirler and produce a magnificent keyboard rendition of Prokofieff's "Sonata #7"—all at the same time.

"Hey, I'm leaving all the work to you," Megan suddenly realized, tossing her letters onto the dining-room table. "There must be something I can do to help."

"Well, there is one thing. Maybe you can tell me if your dad would prefer that I serve apple or grape juice at supper?"

"With chili? As far as Dad is concerned, you can't go wrong with milk." Megan opened the cupboard door and counted out the plates and soup bowls. "Do you want to eat here in the kitchen or in the dining room?"

"The dining room," Libby suggested, then hesitated. "Candles would be nice, too, for Sabbath and all. Your dad told me about the family tradition you've maintained over the years, having lighted candles on the table Friday evening."

Megan's jaw stiffened, then she bit her lip. "Yes, I think candles would be nice tonight. I'll get out the crystal candle holders, the ones Dad gave Mom on their first anniversary, er, I mean . . ."

She felt a gentle hand on her arm. "It's OK." Libby's soft brown eyes read the message Megan struggled to hide. "I know this is tough for you right now. Let's use the brass ones on the mantle instead, all right?"

Tears swam before Megan's eyes as she turned toward the older woman. "Thanks." Megan tried to smile. "Thanks for being understanding." ·

Suddenly her dad burst into the room with Alan close behind. "Hey, what's going on in here—woman talk or something? You girls got a couple of hungry bears on your hands tonight."

Drawing herself up to her full 5′ 4″, Megan whipped about to face her 6′ 3″ father. "Girls? Girls?" she mocked playfully. "Sir, you may refer to us as ladies or, perhaps, women. But we are definitely *not* girls. However, if you are sufficiently repentant, you *boys* may speed things up by setting the dining-room table." Before her father could reply, she shoved the stack of dinnerware into his hands. "And you may wipe that smug little grin off your face, sir."

"Hmmph! Women!" Herb huffed as he exited the kitchen. The two women giggled together as Herb continued sputtering to Alan in the next room. His easygoing banter reassured Megan that, in spite of all the changes in their lives, things between her and her father were comfortingly the same.

"You know," Libby confided, "it was your dad's ability to see humor in almost any situation that first attracted me to him." She removed the pan of cornbread from the oven. "He never seems to get uptight. But then, who am I to tell you about your own father? I'll bet your Alan possesses the same trait."

Megan frowned, then brightened. "Did I tell you that Alan won the National Young Businessmen's Award last year? Three major companies were bidding for him last spring before he chose to go with Conn-Burham Electronics."

"My, it sounds like he's really going places," Libby replied. "If you'll carry the tureen of chili to the table, I'll bring the johnnycake."

At the dinner table, Megan leaned back and listened as her father and Alan dominated the conversation. She enjoyed watching her rancher father surprise and confound the city-wise young man she intended to marry. He could talk stocks, bonds, and CD's as well as any yuppie broker from Boston! *Yep*, she thought, *Dad can hold his own anywhere.*

Libby and Herb shared their plans regarding their upcoming wedding, less than a month away. "Of course, we hope you'll be able to be here, Alan."

An uncertain smile flickered across his face. "I'll do my best, sir." Detecting a strange sadness in his eyes, Megan promised herself to explore the reasons behind his mood swing.

The lively conversation continued well into the evening. The candles melted down to stubs, forming waxy puddles on the brass candle holders. At last Megan's father stood up. "Terrific chili, old gal." He came around to where Libby sat. "Well, son, the ladies made the meal. It's only fitting we clean up afterward. Thank the Lord for electric dishwashers!" He planted a kiss on Libby's upturned cheek. "After we finish, how about you and me taking a walk to the overlook and leave these two young lovebirds alone for a while?"

The twinkle of happiness evident in both Libby's and her father's eyes caused Megan's heart to skip a beat. It was the same spark she'd always admired in the glances between her mother and her dad. *How can he fall in love like that again, and with another woman?* she wondered. *Maybe that's one of the differences between a man's love and a woman's.* She glanced shyly over at Alan. He, too, was watching the kinetic interaction between the couple. *I am sure I could never love another as much as I love this man*, she told herself.

"Why don't you two take the four-wheeler out to the mesa?" Herb suggested. "It's promising to be a gorgeous sunset."

Megan's father was right. The sunset proved to be spectacular. Standing on an outcrop at the edge of the canyon, the couple watched the shadows of night seep into the wrinkles of the canyon's sandstone walls and skitter across the canyon floor until only a soft glow lingered on the horizon.

"Turn your eyes upon Jesus . . ." Megan sang the words to the old familiar chorus while Alan gazed silently into the darkened abyss lying at their feet. "Out here, I feel so in tune with my Saviour. When I was a kid and was upset about something, I would ride my horse, Amby, out here and . . ." She looked over at Alan. "Hey, are you listening? Alan? Hello!" She waved her hand in front of his eyes.

"What?" He snapped to. "Oh, uh, sure, it sounds fine with me."

"Huh? What sounds fine with you?" She frowned and tipped her head to one side. "What's wrong, Alan? You've hardly said two words to me since you arrived. If I did something to upset you, I'm sorry—just talk to me."

"No, I'm the one who should apologize. I guess I've been a little preoccupied." Alan looked everywhere but into Megan's eyes as he ran his hands nervously over her upper arms. "What do you say we head back now? Your dad will send the sheriff after us if we don't get back to the house soon."

His touch held little warmth. She pulled away and hugged her arms about herself. "No, we really need to talk. No relationship can grow when partners refuse—"

But Alan didn't wait to hear the rest of her statement. Without a glance, he turned and strode back down the trail toward the truck.

CHAPTER

2

Megan and Alan drove back to the ranch in silence. The house was dark except for the front-porch lights that guided their steps to the door. Silently they tiptoed into the hall. Without a word Alan kissed Megan goodnight and hurried up the stairs to the guest room.

Something's wrong. Megan said to herself. *I need to get away and think.* She tiptoed up the darkened stairwell and hesitated in front of her bedroom door. In order to house all four adults for the weekend in the three bedroom house, Megan had volunteered to sleep on the sofa and let Libby stay in her room. A shaft of light spilled from beneath the door. *Good,* she thought. *Libby must still be up.* She knocked on the door and whispered, "Libby, are you still awake?"

The door swung open, flooding the hallway with light. "Sure, honey." Libby's form filled the doorway. "How can I help you? Do you need to get something?"

"Yeah—a hooded sweatshirt from the dresser," Megan mumbled and pointed to the highboy across the room.

Libby stepped aside to allow Megan to enter. "Come on in, help yourself." Libby's elegant oriental silk dressing robe and matching nightgown took Megan by surprise. Libby smiled at the younger woman's appreciative gaze. "Do you like it?"

"Yes, very much," Megan replied. "Somehow I would have taken you to be a lace-trimmed flannel-type woman."

Libby shuddered. "Not in this lifetime, if I can help it. I bought this particular set right after my husband, Fred, died. The vibrant reds and blues made me feel alive again."

"I can see why," Megan agreed. *That should teach you not to judge a person too quickly*, Megan scolded herself as she rifled through her

16

bureau drawer. *People are rarely what they seem to be.* For some reason, Alan's face flashed into her mind. She bit her lip and closed the drawer.

"Are you sure you'll sleep all right down there in your father's office?" Libby asked. "I feel terrible pushing you out of your own room."

"Oh no, I'm just fine. I really don't mind at all." Megan glanced down at the sweatshirt in her hand. "Alan went to bed already and I, uh, wasn't tired enough to sleep, so, uh, I decided to take a walk. The stars are incredible tonight."

"Want company or is this a solo jaunt?"

Megan's eyes clouded. She turned her face to the bureau. Taking moonlit walks had been a favorite activity for Megan and her mom. That Libby would want to share it took her by surprise. "Sure, come on along. I'll wait in the kitchen while you change."

Why did I do that? Megan grumbled to herself as she hurried down the stairs. *I really want to be alone—to think. Or do I?* She picked up the letter she'd not yet gotten around to reading—the one from Mrs. McAdams at the library. She glanced through it once, then read it again more slowly. An unsettling fear crept over her. Before she could analyze her concern any further, Libby arrived, decked out in a pair of Levi's, well-worn cowboy boots and a fleecy-wool plaid jacket. "Ready?"

Megan dropped the letter onto the table. "Let's go."

Two flashlight beams bounced ahead of the women as they trotted down the driveway in front of the house. They crossed the county road and hiked up the grassy slope on the other side. When they came over the top, Megan found her favorite boulder and sat down. Libby joined her.

Thousands of stars filled the desert sky, a light show straight from the Creator's hand. "They seem so close, don't they?" Megan whispered. "Like you could just reach up and catch one."

"I know. Somehow, they bring God closer." Libby sat next to her in comfortable silence for a time, watching the ever-changing drama of the skies.

"Imagine, over 100 billion galaxies out there, each with more than a billion stars. And we're such an insignificant part of the entire picture," Megan mused aloud.

"Small perhaps, but never insignificant," Libby replied. "Even the tiniest hummingbird is significant to the Creator. Our problems are His problems." She paused, then added, "Something's bothering you tonight, isn't it?"

Megan shrugged, and kicked at a small rock with the toe of her boot.

"You want to talk about it?"

Megan leaned forward and placed her chin in her hands. "I don't know."

"I'm here if you need me," Libby assured her. "Not as a mother substitute—no one can ever be that," Libby assured her. "But as a friend."

Megan didn't reply. The women watched as a shooting star streaked across the glittering heavens. A coyote howled from atop a faraway bluff.

"Do the questions ever stop?" Megan whispered.

"Questions? What questions?"

Megan sighed. "Questions about the future, about marriage, about the man you've chosen to spend the rest of your life with, even about yourself."

Libby chuckled. "Good question."

Megan stared at the older woman. "You mean you have doubts about marrying my father?"

"Doubts? No, not doubts. But I still have a lot of questions."

"What's the difference?"

"Hmm, another good question . . . " Libby paused. "Perhaps a question is positive while a doubt is negative. Does that make sense?"

"No," Megan answered truthfully, then lapsed into silence again. She thought about Libby and her father. The more she learned about the woman, the more comfortable she became about her father's upcoming wedding. *How ironic*, she thought. *The more I learn about Alan, the less secure I feel. Maybe I'm just having pre-wedding jitters.* "I received a strange letter today," she began, "from a lady I worked with in the college library. While she didn't come right out and say so, she seemed to be trying to tell me something about Alan—sort of a warning or something. It didn't make any sense."

Megan scuffed the heel of her boot through the loose dirt. "I respect Mrs. McAdams very much. She helped me cope after my mom died. I've never heard one word of gossip or even exaggeration come out of her mouth—not ever."

"Have you discussed the letter with Alan?"

Megan shook her head. "I didn't read it until after he'd gone to bed. Even if I had read it earlier, I don't know what I would say. The letter was so vague, not at all like Mrs. McAdams."

"Hmm . . ."

"To top it off, Alan's behaving strangely this weekend, like he has something on his mind. Everything I do irks him. Maybe I'm just overreacting about his moodiness or, even about the letter." She paused. "Yeah, on second thought, it's probably nothing."

Libby remained silent for a few minutes, then spoke. "The Lord speaks to us in many different ways. If you have serious doubts, pray it through. Remember, you're a longtime married."

Megan nodded. Suddenly she felt very tired. Megan turned her flashlight beam on the face of her wristwatch. "Oh my! It's almost midnight."

Libby shook her head. "I didn't realize it was so late."

Megan stood up and brushed the grit from her jeans. "If we don't get some sleep, Pastor Thompson will need to blow whistles and clang bells in order to keep the two of us awake in church tomorrow morning."

Giggling like errant schoolgirls, the two women hurried down the hill to the house and into the darkened kitchen. "Good-night, Megan." Libby whispered from the stairs. "I sure enjoyed the walk."

"Me too." Megan smiled. "We can do it again, real soon." Libby smiled and turned to go up the stairs.

Silently, Megan changed into her nightgown. She spread a blanket on the sofa and turned back the corner. *Boy,* she thought, glancing at the clock once more, *I'm going to sleep like a log.*

But she didn't. Instead, the moment she lay down her eyes popped open. Questions bombarded her mind. Or were they what Libby called doubts? *What is Mrs. McAdams trying to tell me?* Megan rolled back and forth on the narrow sofa. Finally, in desperation, she jumped up and turned on the lamp.

Collecting her letters from the table, she reread the one from Sara. Going to New York City to work as a taskforce social worker right after graduation had been a big leap for Sara, a small-town girl. Obviously, Sara was thriving in her usual wacky style of life in the big city. Megan refolded the letter and slipped it back into its envelope. She glanced down at Mrs. McAdam's letter. If it had been a rattlesnake, it couldn't have looked more deadly to Megan.

OK, I'll read it again. Maybe I missed something the first time through, she thought. She removed the letter from its envelope. Word by word she considered every phrase and inference. Regardless of how she read it, nothing made sense. Exhausted, she stuffed it back into the envelope and turned out the light.

Stretching out on the daybed once more, she stared up at the darkened ceiling. *Please God,* she prayed, *I'm scared. If I am about to make a major mistake in my life, please tell me before the damage is done. If only Mom were here . . .* The memory of her loving, practical mother drifted into her mind, warming her and bringing her a sense of peace.

"Hey, sleepyhead, you gonna' sleep all day?" From outside her slumber, Megan heard her father's voice. "You're gonna' be late for church if you don't get a move on."

Megan sat up and rubbed her eyes. She glanced at the desk clock and gasped. "Eight-thirty! I'll never be ready in time!"

Sabbath school had already begun by the time Megan and Alan parked Beulah and entered the little stucco church. Her father and Libby had gone on ahead in the pickup truck since Herb was to lead the opening song service.

"I hate being late," Megan whispered as they entered the foyer.

"There you are, you little dickins," announced a booming voice. A large, smiling woman engulfed Megan in her abundant arms. "And this must be your intended."

"Yes, this is my fiancé, Alan. Alan Hendricks, I'd like you to meet Reba Cook."

"Well, bless my soul, but isn't he a looker?" The woman patted Alan's cheek affectionately. "You're a mighty lucky young man, you know, to win the love of this Albuquerque buttercup. You'd better treat her right, ya' hear? We're mighty fond of her."

Megan laughed and gave Reba a hug. "You wouldn't be a bit biased, now, would you?"

"Biased? Me? Well, I never." Reba grinned.

"Shouldn't we go in and sit down?" Alan hissed, gripping Megan's elbow.

"I guess you're right." Megan turned to Reba Cook. "We'll talk after the service, OK?"

Megan and Alan entered the sanctuary and found a seat. "She's like something from a Norman Rockwell painting," Alan whispered.

Sensing a note of derision in his voice, Megan replied, "She's a dear, probably one of the most gentle persons I've ever met—truly one of a kind."

"I hope so," Alan mumbled.

Throughout the services, Megan could sense Alan's displeasure. She'd never been embarrassed about the simple, country people she'd grown up around. On the contrary, she'd treasured their support and encouragement, especially after her mother died. While they lacked the polish and sophistication of her college friends, these people had a style of their own—a natural, honest style. *Can't he see that they are a part of who I am?* she wondered. *Maybe, in time.* But it only got worse.

When 87-year-old Grandpa Sanchez presented the mission story and stumbled over the word *Maiduguri,* a city in Nigeria, Alan sneered. When the soprano soloist missed a high note during the special music, he cringed. His attitude deteriorated still further during the church service. By the closing song, Megan's only thought was to get Alan away from her friends as quickly as possible. But that was not to be. Outside the church, a gauntlet of well-wishers lined up to be introduced to Megan Daniels' fiancé.

"You are gettin' yourself quite a woman, there. Take good care of her," Grandpa Sanchez admonished.

Bob Brown grabbed Alan's hand and pumped it with the vigor of an oil field wildcatter. "Great gal ya' got there."

Bonnie Miller regaled the reluctant young man with tales from Megan's dark past. "She scooted from the back row to the front of the church—right under the pews, she did. Her mama couldn't catch her for nothin' until the end of the mornin' prayer. And then there was the time—"

"I think it's time we go, Mrs. Miller," Megan interrupted. "You don't want him to know all of my deep, dark secrets do you?"

Megan skillfully maneuvered the ramrod-straight Alan to her car. "Whew!" she sighed, slipping into the driver's seat. "They can be a bit much, can't they? They've known me since day one. For that matter, Reba Cook almost had to deliver me on the way to the hospital."

When he failed to reply, she glanced toward him. "Alan? Alan, did you hear me? What's wrong?"

"Nothing. I—I . . . nothing."

"OK, if that's the way you want it." She returned her attention to the Interstate's midday traffic. *What is happening?* Megan wondered. *Everything seems to bother him. It's as if . . .* She forced the thoughts from her mind.

On campus, she and Alan had been known as the "happy" couple—the couple who never fought, who never disagreed, who always participated in the campus activities. His interest in spiritual things was what first attracted her to him. Yet, here, today, surrounded by the people that meant so much to her, he was like a stranger to her.

Shimmering mirages danced on the hot road surface as she drove toward home. Clumps of trees or a windmill indicating the occasional farmhouse, broke up the monotony of the sparsely-settled desert landscape. Megan glanced over at Alan's somber profile as he stared out at some far-distant point ahead on the road. She remembered Mrs. McAdams cryptic letter. *Something is definitely wrong*, she decided. *And, one way or another, I will get to the bottom of it before he leaves tomorrow.*

Alan's mood didn't improve over the dinner table. Sensing a problem, Megan's father tried to lighten the situation by sharing stories about Megan's childhood and their daily life on the ranch.

"There's apple cobbler à la mode for dessert," Libby announced as she collected the used dinner plates and silverware.

"Here, let me help," Megan volunteered, removing the platter of left-over roast and the half-empty bowl of mashed potatoes.

Except for Herb's enthusiastic praise for Libby's cobbler, they ate dessert in silence. When Megan finished and started to clear the table, Libby interrupted. "Your dad and I can take care of the dishes. You two run along now, ya' hear."

Megan excused herself. "Alan, there's a ghost town I think you'll find interesting near here. It's called Cerrillos. It's about twenty minutes away. Let's change our clothes and go poke around the old buildings." Alan nodded. He mumbled a thank you to Libby for the meal and disappeared upstairs. When he came down a few minutes later, he and Megan headed for the truck. Megan studied the stranger walking beside her. Even in faded jeans and a plaid shirt, he breathed style. If he'd been wearing Western boots and a Stetson hat he could have stepped out of a men's cologne ad in an issue of GQ.

"Do you want to drive?" Megan dangled the keys in front of him.

"No, you go ahead. You know where you're going." Alan walked around to the right side of the truck and climbed in.

The afternoon sun beat down on the truck as it bounced over the rutted back roads to the abandoned town. For the first ten minutes, Megan attempted to make conversation by pointing out the sights along the way. When she received nothing more than a grunt in response, she stopped trying. Her thoughts ran wild in a jumble of apprehension and concern.

The ramshackled town perched at the base of the Sandia mountain range spoke of an earlier time. Soft spirals of smoke wafted from the chimneys of two or three of the homes. "A few free spirits from the city have become squatters here," Megan explained. She drove down what had once been a busy main street and parked the truck in front of a boarded-up store. The sign swinging in the breeze from one nail above the door read, *Cerrillos General Store.*

Megan and Alan got out of the truck and wandered aimlessly down the wooden sidewalk. Faded signs identified the boarded up businesses: a milliner's shop, a smoke shop, a bar, and the town's only hotel. They peered between the boards into what had once been the sheriff's office. At the back of the dust-coated room, they could see three cells. The iron-barred gates sprawled uselessly on the floor. They made their way to the weather-beaten clapboard chapel at the end of the street. Carefully, they climbed the decaying steps. The front door groaned as if reluctant to admit the intruders.

Megan stepped inside the sanctuary. Except for the evidence of an occasional traveler seeking a night's shelter from the elements, the church was in excellent condition. Someone with a scrub brush and cleanser could have it ready for services in just a few hours. Had it been more than three years since she'd come here for the last time with her mother? It didn't seem so long ago.

"I've always loved coming here," Megan explained as Alan sat down on the back row. She strolled up the center aisle then whirled about in childlike abandon as tender memories flooded over her. "When I was a little girl, I dreamed of getting married in this chapel. My bridesmaids would wear gingham and carry wildflower bouquets." She closed her eyes, imagining the scene. "I'd wear a gown of white organdy and handmade lace. On my head, I'd wear a halo of daisies and English tea roses." She glanced up at Alan. A look of horror swept across his face. She laughed. "Oh, not anymore. Life is much too complicated for something as simple as . . ."

She strolled to the pulpit, then whirled about. "Alan, we've got to talk—now! What is going on?"

Alan was startled at her commanding tone. Guilt and fear flashed across his face. "I-I-I don't know what you're talking about."

"Talking about? You mean, besides the fact that you've hardly spoken to me all weekend."

"I have a lot on my mind," he defended, shoving his hand in his pocket. "I guess my job is getting to me . . ." His voice dropped to a mumble. He stared absently at the floor.

Megan took a deep breath. "I received a strange letter from Mrs. McAdams—you remember Mrs. McAdams at the college library—"

Alan leaped to his feet and started pacing across the back of the church. "That gossiping old biddy! She's always sticking her nose where it doesn't belong! What did she tell you—that she saw me driving through town with Melody Powers?"

Megan stared at Alan. "No, she didn't—"

"Well, she got it all wrong. I ran into Melody at the market and offered her a lift home."

"But, she didn't—"

Oblivious to Megan's reply, Alan ran his hand distractedly through his hair. "Well, who are you going to believe? Her or me?"

"Alan!" She leveled her steel-trap gaze at the man she'd promised to marry. "Mrs. McAdams didn't tell me anything—but perhaps, you should."

Mustering his last vestige of defiance, Alan played stare-down with her for what seemed like an eternity. The silence of the room pounded in her ears to the drumbeat of her heart. Slowly, imperceptively, the belligerence faded from his eyes. His shoulders drooped forward. A sigh escaped his lips as he dropped onto the nearest dusty pew and clasped his head in his hands. "It's a long story. You'd better sit down."

C H A P T E R

3

Megan sat down beside Alan and waited. The dust-ladened air cast sepia tones on the isolated little world inside the desert chapel. An old upright piano, its keyboard and front panels covered with graffiti, cast a forlorn shadow across the wide plank floor. Messages of "Make love—not war" and "Peace at all costs" scarred the faded plaster walls.

"You can't possibly understand what it was like growing up as an anglo in an east Los Angeles barrio," Alan said at last. "I did what I had to do to survive. When I was 12 years old, my good-for-nothing father ran out on me. Then I was adopted by the Hendrickses. It was like winning the lottery. They were rich, had a big house and fancy clothes, and went to Palm Springs on vacation. I knew I was set for life. I would do anything to make Mom and Pop Hendricks happy."

Megan pursed her lips and frowned. "What does all this have to do with us—now? Be honest! I can't stand playing deceitful little games."

Shocked, he looked at her in dismay. "Why, everything! The one thing Mom and Pop wanted more than anything was for their little inner-city refugee to turn Christian. So I did. I got baptized because I knew it would please them. I went to a Christian college to please them; I dated a Christian girl to please them—everything!"

Now it was Megan's turn to be shocked. "A-a-are you saying," she stammered, "that you only asked me to marry you because I fit your picture of a good Christian wife?"

"Yes—well, no, not exactly. I didn't know I was going to fall in love in the process," Alan admitted.

Megan took a deep breath and glanced up at the smoke-scarred ceiling. "And all the great spiritual discussions, all the times we studied the Bible together and talked of one day going as missionaries to South America? That was all for—?"

"No!" Alan defended. "I meant everything I said at the time. It's just that now I'm out of school. I've got money to spend, with no one calling the shots but me. I guess I want to have some fun before I settle down."

"Fun?"

"Yeah, fun!" An edge of defiance entered his voice. "I want to try all the things I could only dream about as a kid. Maybe if I get it out of my system, then I'll return to the straight-and-narrow and stay there."

Megan nodded. "And that's where Melody fits into this equation?"

"Yeah, I guess it is," Alan admitted. "She's one high-class lady who knows how to have a good time."

Megan scuffed the toe of her sneaker across a rough-hewn floorboard. "And where do I fit in—or don't I?"

"Oh, Megan, that's the problem."

She steeled her gaze at him. "Problem? Now I'm a problem . . . " The finality of death swept through her. She closed her eyes to the pain.

Alan rushed to Megan, gently cradling her face between his hands. "Darling, I do love you. Can't you understand? This little rebellion of mine will last only a few months, and when it's over I will want to come back to you." He traced the outline of her lips with his finger. "Please be patient with me. Don't abandon me."

Her eyes flew open. "Abandon you? Really, Alan, who's abandoning whom?" She pulled away. "Let me get this straight. You are asking me to put my life on hold while you sow your wild oats, then come limping back to me." She wrapped her arms tightly about herself and turned away. "As my dad always says: 'When you sow wild oats, you can expect a bumper crop.' Well, brother, I don't want to share in that harvest."

He started to protest, but she waved a finger under his nose. "Do you think what you are asking of me is fair? What kind of a jerk do you take me for? And where does God fit into all of this?"

"Oh, Megan, I'm such a fool." Alan sighed and exhaled slowly. "I never really thought about how this would hurt you. I'm sorry. There won't be any more Melodys or Elaines or—"

"Don't make any promises you can't kee—Elaine? Who's Elaine?"

He reddened and waved his hands defensively. "Oh, she's just a secretary in my office. She doesn't mean anything to me."

A ragged sigh escaped Megan's lips. She shook her head slowly and sank back into the dusty wooden seat. "Oh, Alan, how I wish I could believe you."

Long shafts of golden light from the late afternoon sun streaked through the broken windowpanes and across the chapel floor. Slowly Megan rose to her feet. She suddenly felt worn and tired. "I guess there's nothing more to say. We'd better head back to the ranch now."

Her body moved in slow motion, as if trapped in a nightmare. Somewhere just beyond her consciousness she heard Alan babbling, trying to defend himself. She moved through the motions of climbing into the truck, starting the engine, and putting it into gear. She failed to stop at the town's only intersection. When the driver of a dust-covered pickup laid on his horn, she didn't notice.

"Megan, we gotta talk," Alan insisted. "You're the one who is always saying we need to communicate. So communicate with me."

She stared straight ahead at the asphalt disappearing beneath the truck's wheels. *If only I could pray,* she thought, but her brain seemed numb with shock. *If only I could cry*—but tears refused to fall. She felt so old, so alone. *Oh, Mama,* she wailed on the inside, *if you'd been here this would never have happened.* A dull ache gripped her heart and refused to let go. *Megan,* she silently scolded herself, *how could you have been so blind? Meg*—

"Megan! Hey, Megan," Alan's voice penetrated the thick fog within her brain, "didn't you just pass your driveway?"

"Huh? Oh, yeah." She stopped the truck, jammed the gears in reverse, and turned down the drive.

That evening was like a dream. Herb corralled a huge bowl of popcorn and led a fierce foursome of Uno. It was fun, like old times. Megan could hear herself laughing much too loudly, behaving too raucously, yet she knew that if she stopped, she would dissolve in tears. The questioning glances she intercepted between her father and Libby, the guilt and fear in Alan's eyes, told her she fooled no one with her boisterous acting.

When the clock struck 11:00, Megan excused herself and disappeared without explanation into her father's study. The warm wood tones of the room and the many rows of books lining the walls seemed to reach out to ease her pain. She tried to pray, but a cold angry whirlwind froze out her thoughts. She turned out the light and slipped beneath the puffy down comforter. Tears spilled out on her embroidered white pillowcase. Her weeping turned to sobs.

A knock sounded at the door. "Megan?" her father called. "You OK? Do you want to talk?"

She gulped back her tears. "Not tonight—not tonight."

He hesitated a moment, then said, "You know where to find me if you need me."

"Thanks, Dad," she sniffed.

She tossed about on the sofa, trying to sleep, but to no avail. Her mind spun as she recalled Alan's words. "Don't abandon me. Don't abandon me . . . me . . . me . . . " She finally drifted into a troubled sleep, yet even then nightmares of Alan and Melody disturbed her rest.

The next morning her head pounded. Her eyes ached from too many tears and too little sleep. Herb took one look at her and insisted he drive the also silent Alan to the airport. She readily agreed. She'd been dreading their trip to the airport.

"Why don't you take Libby with you, Dad?" Megan suggested. "You could drop Alan off, then take her to lunch at the Territorial House in Corrales."

As Alan prepared to leave, he promised to call and let her know he'd arrived home safely. He leaned over to kiss her goodbye, but she turned away. He bent down to pick up his overnight case, then straightened. He flinched at the look of disgust in her eyes. "Well, I gotta' go. They're, ah, waiting in the truck for me."

"So go . . ." The ice in Megan's tone surprised even herself. As the screen door slammed behind him, she steadied herself against the stair bannister. "Why, God, why?" she wailed, shaking her head in dispair. "You promised that if I turned my life over to You, You would direct me, guide me, keep me from falling—You would always be with me. Those are Your words, not mine. Well, guess what? I fell flat on my face!"

During the next few hours, she moved zombielike through the empty house. By the time Alan landed in Los Angeles and called to see if she was all right, she knew what she had to do. "I'm sorry, Alan. This is goodbye."

A stunned silence followed. Then he spoke. "Megan, I had time to think about us on the return flight and I know what I want—I want you. I was wrong, I admit it. I don't want a Melody or an Elaine as a life partner, I want you."

Her heart ached as she measured her words. "Sorry, but I don't want you. You need to decide what kind of a life you really want. As for me, I know what I want—I want to have children, not marry one."

Alan pleaded with her. He vowed to settle down, to stop dating other women. "Look, I'll even rededicate my life to Christ if that's what you want."

"If that's what I want?" she shot back. "My heart would love to believe you, Alan, but my head tells me that you spoke the truth back there in the chapel—maybe for the first time. I can't and won't marry you. I'll send your watch back in tomorrow's mail."

"B-b-b-ut—"

"Goodbye Alan, give my love to the Hendrickses. They're wonderful people. And, have a good life." She hung up the receiver and turned off the phone's message machine. The telephone rang at regular intervals for the next hour and a half. Fearing her resolve might weaken, she grabbed a woolen blanket and hiked up to her favorite boulder.

During the afternoon, the weather had deteriorated to match her mood. Stone-faced, she watched as lightning flashed across the western sky. Thunder boomed, echoing the length of the canyon below her. Yet no rain fell. Hours later, her father found her wrapped in a green plaid blanket and staring into the yawning chasm.

Without a word, he sat down beside her and gathered her into his arms. She dissolved into his embrace. "Oh, Daddy, love hurts so much."

"I know, Meggy." He choked back his tears. "I know."

"At least I didn't buy the dress yet or put a deposit on the college chapel. He'd convinced me to be married in California. He planned to invite half the state's population to our wedding." She lapsed into silence. Suddenly she straightened and voiced a new thought. "What I wanted didn't really matter to him. My whole world revolved around his wants, his goals, and his desires." She snuggled back down into her father's embrace.

Ten minutes passed. Her father spoke. "What are you planning to do now?"

"I have no idea. I don't want to stay here in New Mexico and sell. beepers for the next 50 years—that's for sure."

"Well, don't worry about it now. God will show you the way He'd have you go."

"Yeah, sure," she mumbled. She slowly rose to her feet. "We'd better get back to the house. Libby will be worried."

"Don't worry about Libby. She is already on her way back to Tucumcari—and she sends her love."

"She's neat. I really like her."

"She likes you too." Her father stood up and scooped the blanket up into his arms. Together they headed down the pathway.

When they entered the house, the telephone was ringing. Her father glanced questioningly at Megan. She shook her head and climbed the stairs to her room. The telephone continued to ring throughout the evening. Her father warded off Alan's calls as best he could.

As he headed for bed, he stuck his head around the door of her room and said goodnight. "You should talk to him, you know," he advised.

"Why? There's nothing left to say." The telephone jangled again and her father crossed the room to answer it. "Won't he ever give up?" Megan mumbled.

"Megan," her father began.

"No, Dad," Megan insisted, "I won't talk—"

"It's Sara. She's calling long distance."

Megan blanched. "Not now—not Sara, not now." Reluctantly she took the receiver from her father's hand.

"Sara, what a surprise!" In spite of herself, Megan soon found herself laughing. For Sara, city life was one bizarre antic after another. Finally Sara ran down.

"So what's happening with you? Did you get my letter?"

"Uh, yes, I got your letter on Friday. Uh, I was planning to answer it tonight."

"OK, what's up? I can hear it in your voice—something's wrong. Are you suffering from the wicked stepmother syndrome?" Sara was as tactful as a stun gun.

"Oh, no, quite the contrary." Megan chuckled at Sara's terminology. "Libby is great."

"So, what is it? You know you can't hide anything from me."

Megan shook her head and smiled. She never could keep secrets from her roommate no matter how hard she tried. She reached for a box of Kleenex tissues on the nightstand beside her bed and began. Within minutes, she'd revealed the entire fiasco of the weekend and her break with Alan. Silence followed. *Perhaps we've been cut off,* she thought. "Sara? Are you there? Did you hang up on me?"

"No—no, I'm still here. Then, is it really over?"

"Absolutely!"

"Well," Sara began slowly, then picked up speed. "I don't need to tell you that I never trusted that jerk. He always seemed too plastic, like a Malibu Ken doll." Sara paused as if, for the first time since infancy, she was at a loss for words. "I didn't tell you this before because I didn't want to hurt you and it was only hearsay, but during the last few months, Angela and Marti—you remember our next-door neighbors—wrote that they'd seen Alan flitting about town with a number of different girls. His classic Mustang convertible is rather distinctive, you know—especially in a small town."

"I feel like such a fool. Everyone knew except me. Well, it's in the past." Megan took a deep breath and continued. "My biggest problem right now is that my dad's getting married next month. They need time to adjust to marriage without having an adult daughter hanging around. I wish I could go live in a box canyon somewhere and forget the world exists."

"I have a better idea." Sara grew serious. "And don't say no until you've thought about it! Come to New York and live here with me and Mama Grace for a few months. And—there's this gorgeous guy, the youth pastor at the church where I attend, who—"

"Don't be ridiculous," Megan scoffed. "The last thing I need right now is another man in my life. And New York City isn't exactly my idea of a hideaway from the world."

"Uh, well," Sara paused for a moment, "promise to think about it. I have a great idea, but I'll have to get back to you on it."

Megan shuddered. Sara and her great ideas! She remembered the night during their freshman year when Sara convinced Megan and another friend to go through the dorm putting "out-of-order" signs on the bathroom stalls. Their poor half-awake victims were led from one stall to the next, from one bathroom to the next, and from one floor to the next in search of operable plumbing. It was only the first of many such pranks Sara instigated and Megan got dragged into by Sara's determination. "Sara, I won't allow you to get me into another of your hairbrained sche—"

"Hey," Sara interrupted, "we've been talking for over an hour, and on my ticket. I'll get back to you in the next few days. Keep your chin up, ya' hear?" The phone clicked before Megan could protest further.

Megan spent Monday calling potential customers. Since she felt miserable already, she reasoned that she couldn't ruin her day any more by spending it cold calling. Later, she drove to the town mall and bought an outrageously expensive yellow print silk scarf to cheer herself up. It didn't work.

On her way out of the mall, Buelah broke down. Fortunately, Western Communications provided car phones for all its sales representatives—even Beulah got one. Sitting in the stalled car, Megan dialed her father's number.

"Beulah just coughed twice, shuddered, and gave up the ghost, right here in the main intersection by the mall!" Megan explained to her father.

"Just sit tight," he advised, "and I'll be right there to pick you up."

Sit tight, she thought, *sit tight. What else can I do but sit tight?* Tears streamed down her face as she pounded the palms of her hands on the steering wheel. "Beulah! I don't believe you. After all we've been through together, even you betrayed me."

Her father called a tow truck to haul Beulah away. On the way home, he noticed Megan had been crying. Even now a tear trickled down her cheek. "Don't worry, honey," he said. "Beulah just needs a new coil, that's all. She'll be up and running in no time."

"I don't care," Megan shot back. "I never want to see that car again." For a moment Beulah's breakdown seemed to symbolize the bleakness of her entire future. "I trusted; I believed; I loved. I will never, never, ever allow myself to trust again."

Her father shook his head in disbelief. "Megan, it's just a car."

"A car? Who's talking about a car? I'm talking about Alan," she wailed. She crossed her arms defiantly.

"Oh." Her father looked confused for a moment, then brightened. "Well, maybe we can get him a new coil, too. What do you think?"

"Oh, Daddy." Megan rolled her eyes. "Be serious. This really hurts, you know."

"I know, honey." He reached over and squeezed her shoulder. "I just hate seeing my little girl so upset. Can't blame me for trying, can you?"

Megan smiled. "I love you, Daddy."

"I love you, Megan."

When they reached home, Megan hurried into the kitchen to begin fixing supper. Her father called from his study. "There's a message on the answering machine. Do you want to hear it?"

"Not really," she replied pulling a carton of frozen string beans from the freezer. "It's only Alan."

A few minutes later, her father entered the kitchen. He looked worried. "You'd better go listen to the message, Megan. It's Sara."

"What? Is something wrong?" She rushed into the den and pressed the button on the answering machine.

Megan listened to the recorded message once, twice, three times.

". . . Mrs. Iverson, the teacher for grades one to four, was rushed to the hospital last night. The doctor says she must stay off her feet for the rest of the pregnancy or she'll lose the baby. They've called all over the East Coast trying to find someone to fill in until the end of the term, with no luck. They want you, Megan, to finish out the school term. Call me back—no matter how late it gets."

Megan returned to the kitchen. She opened a box of frozen corn and dumped it into a pan to heat on the stove. "I can't go to teach school in New York City." Her voice wavered. "I'm not a teacher. I'm an English major. I want to write for a living or edit books—not teach!"

Megan's father set the table in silence. "New York City, Lord?" he muttered. "Why New York City?"

"What?" Megan caught only her father's last word.

"Oh," he sighed and pursed his lips. "Nothing, child. Nothing."

Megan poured the corn into a serving bowl and set it with a thump onto the table. "I'm not going and that's that!" She whirled about and stomped from the room, sputtering all the way. "If Sara thinks she can push me around like some kind of rag doll, she is crazy!" Megan muttered on about Sara and her harebrained schemes; about trying to sell sophisticated telecommunications systems to hayseed cowboys; and about the irresponsibility of men in general—Alan in particular— all the way upstairs to her bedroom.

When the telephone rang, Megan eyed the extension phone on her night table warily. On the third ring, she grabbed the receiver from its cradle and growled. "Alan, I've had a lousy day. Beulah died. A tacky businessman made a pass at me and I'm moving to New York City, now leave me alone!"

"Hello?" A surprised male voice spoke up from the other end of the line. "My name is Mike Feldman, uh, Pastor Mike Feldman from Brooklyn, New York. I'm trying to reach Megan Daniels. Is—is she there?"

Megan's eyes widened in embarrassment. She covered her mouth in horror. "Oh." She cleared her throat and tried to remember exactly what she'd said. For a moment she was tempted to pretend to be someone else—anyone else. But finally she spoke. "This is Megan Daniels."

"Oh, perhaps I caught you at a bad time, Miss Daniels. I can call back tomorrow if it would be more convenient for you."

"No, no, anything I have to say might as well be said tonight." She listened as Pastor Feldman explained the school's need and Sara's suggested solution. "Uh," he paused again. "Miss Panetta assures me that you have the patience and temperament for such a task."

She chuckled at his carefully chosen phrasing. "Well, I have to admit, you've already heard the worst side of me." Megan asked several questions of her own, especially about making arrangements to fly home to attend her father's upcoming wedding. Getting more or less satisfactory answers, she requested a few days to think it over. The pastor agreed. The telephone receiver fell back into its cradle.

"You're going, aren't you?" Her father's voice startled her back to reality. He'd been standng in the doorway for some time. "I didn't mean to eavesdrop, but I did."

Megan glanced toward him and noted the tears filling his eyes. "Yes." She sat down on the edge of her white canopied bed. She clutched her worn and tattered Pooh bear to her chest. "Yes, I guess, I am."

"New York City." Her father shook his head and walked from the room. "Why New York City, Lord?"

Brilliant sunlight reflected off the plane's silver wings into the surrounding blue sky. A mattress of white puffy clouds obscured the world below. Only an occasional flash of lightning betrayed the lack of tranquility below. The few hours of relative quiet on this, the last leg of her flight to New York, gave Megan time to think; to sort through and analyze her reactions to the events of the last week. A voice from the intercom broke through her meditations.

"We will be landing on schedule at JFK International Airport in New York City," the pilot announced. "We will experience turbulence as we break through the cloud cover . . . "

I've done it now, Megan clutched the airline pillow until her knuckles turned white. She felt her face flush and an unfamiliar sense of terror prickle at the back of her neck.

Oh, Father, she prayed silently as the plane jounced about.

I don't know where You and I goofed as far as Alan is concerned, but I can't pull off this latest mess I've gotten myself into without You. I have to believe You will be with me, just like You promised—to the uttermost parts of the earth. And, she added ruefully, *New York City has to be the most uttermost part of this planet.*

Megan pressed her nose to the window as the plane traced lazy circles over the city. The heavy autumn clouds along the East Coast had lifted. The last shafts of daylight endowed even the humblest of buildings with windows of gold. Her heart beat wildly at the sight of the Empire State Building and the famous twin towers. *So many people living down there,* she thought, *and I'm about to become one of them.* She clutched the pillow to her stomach to still the wildly fluttering butterflies trapped within.

The moment the plane's wheels scraped the runway's surface, the man on the aisle seat next to her leaped up and removed his briefcase and coat from the overhead locker. By the time the plane stopped beside the terminal, he, along with every other impatient passenger had jammed the aisle. The shuffling line of people crowded each other from all sides. The air seemed thick and stale. Megan fought to control a rising panic—claustrophobia. *Get a grip, lady,* she told herself. *Crowds are something you will have to get used to if you plan to survive this adventure.* She leaned back and closed her eyes. Her panic subsided.

Megan decided to remain in her seat until the last person had gotten off the airplane. *If Sara has to wait a few extra minutes for me, too bad,* she thought. *After all, she's the one who got me into this mess in the first place.*

Most of the travelers had headed for the baggage claim area by the time Megan stepped out of the portable causeway into the waiting area. Only a few stragglers lingered—none of whom she recognized. *Great!* she thought. *Alone in one of the biggest airports in the world! Sara, when I get my hands on you . . .*

She spied a paging phone and headed toward it. But on her way, a man slipped in and reached the phone first. She paused a few feet away as he spoke to the operator. *So this is what a New Yorker looks like,* she mused. He was dressed in blue jeans and a YALE sweatshirt. Dark brown, unruly curls gave him the air of having just stepped out of his morning shower. He had a friendly face with laugh lines crinkling at the edge of his deep-set brown eyes. *Probably an ax murderer,* she told herself.

While she waited, she glanced about the busy corridor. *What a strange mixture of humanity,* she thought. Garishly dressed punk rockers and disheveled students vied for space with stylish business-men and camera-ladened vacationers as they rushed to and from the airline waiting areas. *Not a single pair of cowboy boots or a Stetson hat in sight,* she mused. Recalling a favorite scene from the *Wizard of Oz,* she quoted, " 'Well, Toto, looks like we're not in Kansas anymore'—or New Mexico, for that matter!"

"Did you say something to me?" The young man at the telephone was speaking to her.

"No." Megan shook her head and glanced about nervously. "Uh, I just need to page someone."

"Well, have at it." He smiled and held out the telephone receiver toward her. "I'm done." His eyes skimmed over her momentarily and rested back on her face.

"Thank you." She lifted one eyebrow, warily. She reached for the receiver, but the man continued to gaze at her expectantly. "Excuse me." Megan was beginning to feel uncomfortable. "You are done, aren't you?" Startled, the man blinked a moment. A deep-red blush crept up his neck and face and disappeared into the crop of tousled curls resting on his forehead.

"Uh, I-I-I didn't mean to, well, you know. It's just that I'm looking for a girl—"

Megan's steely gaze froze him mid-sentence. "Oh, that's an original—"

"No-no, you misunderstand," he stumbled over his words, eager to explain. "I'm supposed to meet someone who I've never met and I'm starting to panic a little. I've already mistakenly approached at least four women—one who threatened to report me to airport security. He paused, giving her a final going over, "I might as well make you number five. You wouldn't be Meg—"

"Megan Daniels," a voice over the public address system droned, "Megan Daniels, meet your party at the baggage reception area."

The man glanced at her, then toward the loudspeaker, and back again at her. "You *must* be Megan Daniels," he begged. "Oh, please tell me you're Megan Daniels from Albuquerque, New Mexico."

"I am, but who are you?"

Relief flooded the man's face. "Oh, praise God. I finally caught up with you." He grabbed her hand and pumped it enthusiastically. "Sara would have had my head off if I'd somehow missed you."

Megan's eyes narrowed. "Do you have any ID or anything that would connect you to Sara?"

"Come on, Miss Daniels, what do you think I am, an ax murderer?" Megan shot him an icy glare. "All right, for the record—" He reached in his pocket and pulled out his wallet and driver's license. "My name is Michael J. Feldman. I'm the youth pastor at the Brooklyn Eastside Church. But then you already know all that because we talked on the phone last week, arranging this whole trip. Your friend, Sara Panetta, asked me to pick you up since she had to work late today. Satisfied?"

Megan relaxed. A hint of a smile crossed her face. "Nice to meet you, Pastor Feldman." She held out her hand in greeting. A broad smile flashed across his face, and a pleasant glint of amusement played in his eyes. "Well, I don't see anything funny about my wanting some ID," she stated defensively. "A woman can't be too careful—alone in a strange city."

"Apparently that's what those four women I mistook for you thought," he shrugged. He took her carry-on case from her arm and escorted her down the crowded corridor. "It's a wonder I didn't get clubbed with a bowling ball or something. I do apologize, Miss Daniels, if I gave you a start. I'm not usually that—"

"That obvious?" she smirked.

Again he blushed.

"Hey, it's OK, Pastor Feldman," she assured him. "I'm only joking. And please, call me Megan."

He grinned. "If you'll call me Mike."

By the time they picked up her luggage and hiked to his car, Megan felt like she'd known the young preacher for some time. *I hope Sara is smart enough to latch onto this guy,* she thought as she cast another covert glance at his profile. He wasn't exactly handsome. At least, not like Alan's carefully groomed image of the young, upcoming executive. *How would I classify his looks,* she wondered. *A down-home sort of guy—that is, until he smiles. Then wow!*

Now it was her turn to blush. While she missed everything he'd been saying, she didn't miss the bemused expression in his eyes when he turned and caught her staring at him. *Yes,* she decided, *I will definitely need to set a fire under Sara regarding this one.*

As he drove through the tangled maze of rush-hour traffic, he entertained her with anecdotes of city living. His calm, easy-going manner as he maneuvered the automobile through the rush-hour traffic amazed her. If she were driving, her nerves would be completely shot. When a traffic light forced him to stop, Mike reached across the car to the glove compartment and asked, "Want a kiss?"

"Excuse me?" Megan's eyes widened with surprise.

"Do you want a kiss? O-oh!" He reddened and quickly pulled his hand out of the glove compartment. "Uh, uh, a Hershey kiss, I mean." He held out a small plastic bag of foil covered chocolate drops. Megan struggled to keep from laughing while he frantically tried to explain. "One of the kids at the church school thought you might like a little snack on the way and . . ."

She could contain herself no longer, and burst out laughing. Surprised, Mike started laughing too. By the time the light changed to green, tears of mirth rolled down both of their faces. The blaring of car horns behind them brought them back to reality. Mike pulled ahead.

"This isn't even funny!" Mike gasped for breath. "What are we laughing at?"

Megan wiped a tear from her cheek. "I can't wait to tell my dad about this," she laughed. "I meet a city pastor for the first time and right off he's trying to give me a kiss." She opened one of the silver wrappers and popped the candy into her mouth. She then carefully smoothed and folded the foil wrapper in half. "I'm going to keep this either as a memento or for blackmail, whichever suits my fancy." He chuckled and made a grab for the wrapper, but missed.

"Don't tamper with the evidence, sir," she teased, stuffing the foil into her shoulder bag.

Swarms of vehicles crawled through the city streets. They were only a few blocks from Mama Grace's place when Mike said, "I don't know how much Sara has told you about your landlady. She is one remarkable woman. Over the past few years, Mama Grace has raised—oh, I would guess, some 30 or 40 foster children. She has seven living with her now, not including you and Sara."

"*Seven* kids?" Megan's tone elevated in surprise.

"Just wait, you'll see." He laughed. "Mama Grace will adopt you into her brood the minute you walk through her front door. She's a big old mother hen with an even bigger heart."

Mike's description of the woman fell far short of reality. The moment Megan's foot touched the front steps of the massive red brick row house, she found herself engulfed in a set of mahogany brown arms, so strong and so big, she feared she might be smothered with affection. Mama Grace's smile could have given even jolly Saint Nick a lesson in joy.

The woman drew Megan into the brightly lit entryway. Curious faces of every color peered out at her from behind the partially opened doors lining the hallway.

"Come on out here and meet the new teacher, you little imps," the woman called. She turned to Megan. "They've been badgering me all day as to when you would get here. Must say, you made good time through the rush hour traffic, Michael. You can take Miss Daniels' luggage up to the front bedroom on the right—you don't mind sharing a room with Sara, now do you?"

Megan stared in amazement. She had never met anyone who talked so *fast.* She needed to listen intently in order to keep up with Mama Grace's barrage of questions. *Even motor-mouthed Sara must be daunted by this lady,* Megan thought. By now, all seven of the children, ranging between the ages of 5 and 15, surrounded her. The two youngest peeked out at her from behind Mama Grace's voluminous blue skirt.

"I can take your travel case upstairs for you." An ebony-faced teenage boy reached for her case.

"Megan meet Alvin—my number one, main-man," said Mike. With a beaming smile, Alvin followed Mike up the long carpeted staircase with the rest of Megan's luggage and disappeared around the corner. Megan stood in the foyer, a dozen questioning eyes focused on her.

One by one, Mama Grace introduced each of the children. "We're sure glad to have you here, honey," the woman assured her, "what with Mrs. Iverson being rushed to the hospital and all. I did my best with them, but with all my work here, well, there's only so much one person can do."

"I'm not sure I'm cut out to be a teacher," Megan confessed.

Mama Grace wrapped a free arm about Megan's shoulder and gave her a hug. "Ah, you'll do just fine, honey—just fine."

Mike bounded down the stairs with his buddy, Alvin, close behind. "Do we have time before dinner to give Megan a tour of the school?"

"Are you inviting yourself to supper tonight, Pastor Feldman?" Mama Grace asked in mock surprise.

"Oh, uh. Well, I thought . . ." Mike ran his fingers through his hair. He glanced at Megan and smiled self-consciously. "If that's all right?" Mama Grace patted his arm and laughed.

"Of course it's all right. I have a big kettle of lentil stew bubbling on the stove right now and homemade bread still cooling on the breadboard. And yes, you two go ahead over to the school—Sara won't be home for at least an hour and a half."

When Megan reached the relative serenity of Mike's car, she asked, "Do all New Yorkers talk as fast as Mama Grace?"

Mike nodded and grinned. "Most of them do. Before long, you will too. That charming little Southwestern drawl of yours will have completely disappeared."

"What drawl?" she sputtered. He laughed again and eased out into the busy traffic.

Throughout the short drive to the school, Megan stared out the car window at the many people rushing home after their day's work. Women carried shopping bags filled with fresh produce, old men pulled wire shopping carts behind them, kids strutted across the intersections. Everyone had someplace to go and they were in a mighty big hurry to get there.

Mike parked in front of a large brick church. "Well, here we are."

She glanced at the church, then back at him. "The school is in the church?"

"Yep. The two classrooms are in the basement."

She gazed about the street and at the tiny plot of green grass in front of the church. "Where do the kids play?"

"There's a large recreation room too—you'll see." He led her down a narrow gangway to a side door. Beads of perspiration popped out on her forehead as she struggled to control a brief attack of claustrophobia. When they stepped inside the darkened building, Megan shivered.

Mike sensed her discomfort. "Before you jump to any conclusions you ought to know there's a lot of serious educating going on in these rooms. It may seem like a bizarre arrangement, but there's a lot of love being given out here."

"Hey, I didn't—"

"I just wanted you to know. The constituents of this school are proud of the education their children are getting here."

"Oh, no, please don't misunderstand," Megan pleaded. "I know that it isn't the building or the equipment that determines learning, it's the people. Maybe that's what scares me so." The dark little room came to life with the flip of a wall switch. Brightly colored posters covered with childish scribbles decorated the sunshine-yellow walls, like an oasis of color and peace. In spite of her own insecurity, Megan's mind raced with ideas as she walked up and down the aisles, her hand trailing over the desktops as she passed.

"I'll pick you up tomorrow morning at 7:15," Mike said. "School starts at 8:00, but you'll need some time to meet Sam Caggio, the principal, and the other teacher. He'll help you get started. I've been helping him with the seventh and eighth grade Bible classes each morning to give him time to do his administrative duties each day."

Mike kept on talking, but Megan barely heard him. *Tomorrow,* she thought, *each one of these tiny little desks will be filled with a little person expecting great things of me.* "I don't know, Lord," she whispered. "I'm not sure I'm up to this after all. Two weeks ago, I never would have imagined I'd be . . ." She bit her lip as a picture of Alan flashed through her mind.

Mike placed his hand on her shoulder. "You'll do fine. They're great kids. They'll love you."

41

Megan took a deep breath. "I hope so . . ."

They returned to Mama Grace's, each lugging a stack of textbooks and workbooks. After supper Mama Grace took charge of the children, who still seemed very curious about Megan. "Now, kids, you'll have lots of time to get acquainted with the new school teacher. You each have your jobs to do, then comes homework. So scoot!" The children obeyed immediately. Turning to Mike, Mama Grace continued her instructions. "Pastor Feldman, I know you have responsibilities to fulfill also, and you girls," speaking to Sara and Megan, "have to get settled."

"Er," Mike stammered, "I do have a few things I should do this evening. Delicious supper, Mama Grace. Goodnight Sara, Megan." With a little wave he headed for the door, Mama Grace close behind. There was no question who was in charge of this household.

As the two old friends climbed the stairs to their room, Megan whispered, "I feel like my academy dean just announced study hall."

"Mama Grace is a softy, you know." Sara led the way to a large airy room in the front of the house. "She comes across crusty on the outside, but inside, she's whipped cream."

Megan admired the soft yellow rosebud and cornflower pattern in the wallpaper and the matching cornflower blue quilts on the two single beds. A desk stood between the two narrow floor-to-ceiling windows on the front wall. White cotton priscilla curtains fluttered in the breeze coming through the open windows. A comfortable looking rocker and a floor reading lamp in one corner promised to become a favorite retreat for Megan. While she unpacked her suitcases, Sara cleared out space in the dresser drawers and in the closet for Megan's belongings. "We are going to have a fabulous time together, do you know that?"

Megan grinned at Sara's enthusiasm. It was good to be together again. She hadn't realized just how much she'd missed her wonderfully wacky roommate. Sara spent the next two hours filling Megan in on everything she needed to know about big-city living.

"It all sounds very exciting," Megan said at last. "But at the same time kind of intimidating. How do you remember it all?"

"You get used to the pace of everything after a while," Sara replied. "But if you need anything, just ask. I can tell you anything you want to know."

"OK, I have a question."

"Already?"

"Tell me about you and Mike Feldman."

Sara stared at her in surprise. "There's nothing to tell. We're friends, of course, but that's it. As nice as he is, there's just no spark between us."

"Aw, come on," Megan cajoled. "This is your old roomie talking. You can tell me."

"No, really—honest." Sara raised her hands in denial. "And it's not from lack of trying. The entire church congregation has been playing matchmaker since the day I arrived." Sara paused and studied Megan's face. A sly grin crossed her face. "Why? Are you interested?"

Megan blushed uncomfortably. "Sara! You know better than that. Less than a week ago, I broke up with the man I thought I was going to spend the rest of my life with."

"So?"

"So, I trusted Alan and I trusted my own judgment. Both let me down. I have no intention of making that mistake again—not for a long, long time, at least."

"Hey, Alan's a jerk, what do you want?" Sara waved her hands about to demonstrate her disgust.

Megan's smile faded; she picked at her fingernails. "I"—she could feel the tears surfacing—"I want to stop hurting, Sara. I want to stop hurting."

"Aw, kiddo, I'm so sorry." She pulled Megan into her arms and held her tight. "Go ahead and cry. I'm here for you whenever you need me."

"I've always tried to do what is right. I've always tried to do things God's way." Megan's voice wavered. "I'm so angry at myself for getting into the relationship in the first place. I don't know what went wrong. I prayed to God over and over about Alan. Why didn't He stop me right away from falling in love. He knew Alan, and He knew what would happen."

"Hmmph!" Sara snorted. "I don't understand what you are complaining about. It sounds to me like God did stop you from messing up your life. Believe me, and I know what I'm talking about, you aren't hurting anywhere near as much tonight as you would be if you hadn't discovered Alan's cheating until after the wedding."

"But how can I ever trust my own judgment with the next man I find myself attracted to?" Megan shook her head emphatically. "No, no, I won't be that stupid again."

Sara's lips formed a thin straight line; her eyes narrowed. "Look here, if you want a guarantee, go buy yourself a dishwasher. They come with a five-year warranty. Unfortunately, people don't. That's life—face it!"

Megan couldn't believe the change in Sara. She'd never seen Sara so serious, almost distant. "I work every day with people who live with real problems—alcoholism, drugs, rape, physical and sexual abuse—humans balancing on the edge of hell." Sara paused a moment. "You and I are two very lucky women. Just the fact we haven't completely messed up our lives by the ripe old age of 22 gives us an advantage over most of our sisters. I have one case—Becky, a 9-year-old girl, who is pregnant with her father's child. Nine-years-old! She's been abused in every way imaginable. Now Becky has troubles—you and I have inconveniences."

"I-I-I'm sorry. You're right, of course," Megan stammered, "but I still hurt."

Sara squeezed Megan's hand. "I didn't mean to be unkind."

"No, I needed that," Megan brushed a tear from her cheek.

Sara glanced down at her watch and gasped. "It's after midnight! My next lecture of the evening is on the topic of getting enough rest. You are going to suffer from one incredible case of jet lag in the morning, girl."

The next morning the house was a whirlwind of activity. Mama Grace cajoled, threatened, teased, and generally herded the children through their morning chores. After a three-minute shower and a hurried breakfast, Megan grabbed the lunch bag with her initials crayoned on the side and ran outside where Mike was waiting in the car.

"Don't the children ride with us?" she asked as she closed the door.

"No, they'd get to the school too early," Mike yawned. "Besides, the church is only two stops on the subway." Ten minutes later they pulled up in front of the church.

From the moment she stepped out of Mike's car, Megan found herself the center of attention. Sam Caggio was a neat, graying, funny little man who, it appeared to Megan, genuinely enjoyed his job. He walked Megan through the daily routines, showing her the facilities and supplies she would be using. She spent the rest of the morning getting acquainted with each of her students, with the textbooks, and the idea of teaching 32 classes to 15 wiggly bundles of energy.

By the time the last first grader shyly hugged her goodbye, Megan was certain her brain would burst. "If I had had any idea teaching was so complicated," she muttered as she straightened the papers on her desk. Suddenly, she sensed someone watching her from the doorway. Megan whirled about. "Oh," she gasped, "it's only you."

"Only me?" Mike shook his head, his lower lip protruding into a pout. "Already you take me for grant—"

"Never!"

He laughed. "Ready to go?"

During the short drive home, Megan asked, "Are you sure it isn't inconvenient for you, driving me to school and home again like this? I could ride the subway with the children."

"You could, but as long as I have to go right by Mama Grace's anyway, I might as well save you the frustration of riding the rails." Mike watched Megan out of the corner of his eye. "How would you like to tour part of the city on Sunday? We could take in Ellis Island, the Statue of Liberty, and maybe, even the Empire State Building if you'd like?"

"I'd like that and I know Sara would too. Let's do it."

Megan noticed that his grin faded somewhat at the mention of Sara joining them, but she didn't care. The last thing she wanted was for Mike, pastor or no pastor, to get the wrong idea. And for her, at least, dating was definitely the wrong idea!

CHAPTER

5

Megan leaned back in the easy chair and sighed. The stack of workbooks seemed to grow instead of dwindle. Suddenly Sara burst into the bedroom. She threw her purse and briefcase on her bed and danced about the room. "I still can't believe that you're really here. All day long I was afraid I'd dreamed the whole thing. I was so afraid you wouldn't come." Her voice softened. "It's just that I wanted you to come so badly, I was sure something would go wrong at the last minute." Sara threw her arms around Megan and hugged her tightly. "I'm sorry. I get so lonely sometimes."

Megan told Sara about Mike's proposed outing. Sara shook her head. "Two's company; three's a crowd, remember?"

"Sara, I know what you're up to," Megan warned. "Talk about the church members matchmaking! If you don't go on Sunday, I don't go."

"Oh, all right." Sara groaned. "I'll go, but I won't like it!"

Megan had little time to worry about Sara. Her first week of teaching was days of struggle, trying to stay ahead of her students. She was pleasantly surprised to discover that after the first two days, she already considered them *her* kids. There was Cheri, whose eyes bore traces of profound sadness, far beyond her years; Kurt, who, if there was any trouble around, found it; Beth, who lived to please the new teacher; and Lydia, whose energy increased as the day wore on and Megan wore out.

Ah, Lydia, Megan thought. Just that morning, 8-year-old Billy told Megan that Dina had said a "dirty word" during recess. "I didn't say anything bad, Miss Daniels," little Dina responded innocently.

Hmm, Megan thought. *Now I have a problem.* "Dina, could you tell me just what Billy might have heard you say?"

The little girl's eyes brightened with relief. "Sure. I said, 'Billy and Annie sitting in a tree, . . .'"

Megan choked back a grin when she heard Dina's bawdy variation to the familiar children's rhyme. "Dina, where did you learn that word?"

"What word, Miss Daniels?" The little brown-eyed girl smiled sweetly into Megan's face.

"The one that tells what Billy and Annie were supposed to be doing in the tree," Megan explained, not wanting to actually use the term.

"You mean—" Dina replied enthusiastically. Upon hearing the four-letter word, everyone in the class looked up from their books.

"Yes, er, that's the one," Megan nodded. "Do you know what that word means?"

The child grinned with delight. "Yep, it means they were kissing." The child's innocence took Megan's breath away.

"No, honey, it doesn't mean kissing. It's a very bad word that your mommy and daddy wouldn't like to hear you say."

The little girl started to cry. "But Lydia said—"

"It's all right, honey. You didn't know any better. Just never, ever use that word again, OK?" Megan sent Dina back to her seat. *Yes, Lydia could be a real challenge sometimes,* Megan thought to herself. She would have a talk with Lydia in the morning.

On the drive home from school, she told Mike the story. "To think that a little 9-year-old would already have learned such a word! I doubt if she even knows what it means."

The traffic light changed to red, causing him to slam on the brakes. "Don't be too hard on Lydia. She's the youngest of five children, you know. Three of them brothers." The light switched to green and the car lurched forward. "Many of those little kids have had a rough time growing up. Some of their stories would make you cry. Maybe you found a mission today, Megan. You could make an incredible difference in their lives."

She thought about his words for the rest of the ride home. Could teaching be what God wanted her to do with her life? Or was it a stopgap until she could get her life back together? She glanced over at Mike. "What about you?" she asked. "What's your mission—besides being ordained, of course?"

They turned onto the block where Mama Grace lived and pulled up beside the only parking spot available. He jockied the car back and forth until he'd squeezed into the space. Turning off the engine, he released his seat belt. Then he paused.

"In answer to your question, I don't know yet. Wherever God needs me. Maybe working with teenagers." Mike gazed out at the busy sidewalk. "He'll tell me when He's ready."

Alan's face suddenly flashed across Megan's mind followed by a dull ache in her stomach. She flushed and clenched her fists. As Mike turned to retrieve her stack of workbooks from the back seat, their eyes met. Flustered, she dropped her gaze. Her hands trembled as she struggled to release her seatbelt buckle. It refused to open. Mumbling something about her jacket being caught in the clasp, she wrestled with it some more.

"Let me help you." Their hands touched, his on hers, as they both struggled with the belt. She tensed. "Megan, is something bothering you?"

She felt, rather than saw his gaze. "I just can't get this stupid belt off." She slipped her hands away from his and shrank against the car door. "You do it. I'm just complicating things."

A second later he'd released the clasp and the seat belt slid into its holder. Megan quickly opened the door and got out. "Thanks for the ride, Mike," she said briskly. "I've got to go now."

He stared in surprise. "Hey, you forgot your books." He leaped out of the car and circled around to where she stood.

Her heart sank. *Dumb,* she thought. *You're really great at exit scenes, aren't you?* Reluctantly she turned around and reached for the stack of books. Mike pulled back. "Let me carry them in for you."

"No, no, I can do it. I can do it." She took the books and hurried up the walkway.

"Hey," he called after her, "if you ever need to talk, I'm a great listener." Megan rushed inside without responding to his offer.

"I'm sure you would be," she muttered under her breath as she closed the door behind her. She dashed upstairs to her room. "And then you'd get the wrong idea about us and I'd be even more messed up than I am now!"

Placing the books on the desk, Megan carefully pulled the edge of the curtain back and looked out. Mike walked around the car to the driver's side and opened the door. He paused, then looked up. Megan jerked back. The curtain slowly fluttered back into place.

On Megan's first Sabbath, the members of the church held a special potluck to welcome her. She enjoyed meeting the children's parents. Each one thanked her for coming to New York and saving their school. "We really didn't know what we were going to do," Pastor Ulrich admitted. "I didn't realize there was such a teacher shortage."

It surprised Megan to discover how much the people in the small, inner-city church resembled the simple country folk she'd grown up around in New Mexico. Dedication to service, commitment to the family, love of their Saviour, and a desire to finish the work and go home—it was all there. *I guess it's true,* she decided. *No matter where you go, the Christian family presents more similarities than differences.*

Following the potluck, Megan joined the group visiting a nearby nursing home. From there, the teens split off from the main group to go to a park and hand out leaflets, with Mike, Megan, and Sara tagging along as sponsors. Once the pamphlets were all gone, they sat on the grass and sang songs.

Megan leaned against a tree trunk and watched the sun disappear behind a forest of tall buildings. The sweet tones of the familiar chorus "Allelujah" filled her with peace. An image of her mother flickered across her memory. She thought of Alan and sighed. Everything had changed so fast. *Will I ever feel totally normal again?* she wondered, forcing his face from her mind. After worship the group went over to Mama Grace's for an evening of table games.

Being with a group of young people did wonders for Megan's spirits. They laughed and joked with each other, filling the room with a warm, happy glow. Before they knew it, the clock in the hallway began striking 11:30 p.m. Hoarse and exhausted, Mike called it quits.

"You guys gotta' get home before curfew," Mike reminded his teenage charges. "As for you two"—he glanced over at Megan and Sara— "I'll be here around 9:00 tomorrow morning."

"Nine?" Megan grimaced and shook her head. "Not a minute before 10:00—do you hear?"

"Yes, Ma'am." He snapped to attention and saluted. A lopsided grin ruined his proper military pose. "10:00 it is." With a final wave, he was gone.

Precisely at 10:00 the next morning, Megan spotted Mike's blue Toyota pulling up in front of the house. She tugged on her jeans and yanked a red jersey over her head. Running a brush through her hair, she dashed downstairs to the kitchen. Less than two steps behind, Sara followed, still tucking her striped T-shirt into her faded jeans. Mama Grace was already busily at work preparing the family meal.

Mike strode into the room. "Yum! What's cooking?" he sniffed at the tempting aroma of the fresh baked muffins Mama Grace was pulling from the oven.

"Forget it, Mike," Megan laughed. "We're supposed to be going on a tour, remember?"

"You're not going anywhere until you get something to eat," Mama Grace was insistent. "New York's done without you this long. It can wait a little longer."

"My thoughts exactly!" Mike nodded, and took a king-sized bite from a steaming muffin. "Mmmm," his eyes lit up. "These are wonderful, Mama Grace."

Even though they weren't that hungry, Megan and Sara each managed to gulp down a bran muffin and a glass of milk.

"Better take a sweater or a jacket," Mike warned, as he headed for the door. "It can be breezy by the water."

"Good idea." Megan flew up the stairs. "And I'd better take a camera too."

Sara shouted behind her, "Can you grab my brown sweater too, please? The one with the pearl buttons."

"Sure, no problem." Megan ran into the room and pawed through her dresser drawer until she found her favorite black pullover. Sara's sweater was hanging by the door.

"We'll be waiting outside," Sara called.

When Megan reached the car, she noted the seating arrangements and frowned. Mike up front, Sara in the back. *Hmm! This isn't working out right,* she thought. *Sara was supposed to keep this from looking like a date.* For an instant she considered climbing into the back with Sara, but decided against it. She hopped in front and closed the car door. Mike smiled.

"I decided to drive instead of taking the subway since we might want to head into the city before the day is over," Mike explained, easing the Toyota from its parking space.

"Into the city?" Megan looked at him and laughed. "I thought we were already in the city."

Sara leaned forward, her arms resting on the two bucket seats. "The city around here, my dear country bumpkin, is Manhattan."

Megan grinned and rolled her eyes. "So I'm to play the part of the country rube today, is that it?" She looked out the front window. "OK, I'll go along. What's that over there? The famous Brooklyn Bridge?"

Both Mike and Sara laughed. "Afraid not," he explained, "that's the Varazzano-Narrows Bridge. When it was completed, it bumped the San Franscisco's Golden Gate out of being the world's longest suspension bridge." Mike guided the little car through the maze of streets and into the Brooklyn Battery Tunnel. "Hang on, here we go."

Megan looked askance at the cream-colored ceramic tiles lining the tunnel. She felt a familiar tightening in her throat and chest and shivered. "I sure hope the 'big one' doesn't come now."

"The 'big one'?" Sara teased. "We're in New York remember, not California."

"Don't be too smug, dear friend," Megan countered. "I've been reading up on seismic activity around the United States. Can you imagine what would happen if even a little quake rattled Brooklyn's brick buildings for 30 seconds or more?"

"We're headed for Wall Street," Mike said. "A lot of moving and shaking goes on there every day." Up one street, turn, then down another. Megan was thankful Mike knew where he was going. After a short time, he parked the car on a side street. Up ahead, she could see the towering skyscrapers.

They got out of the car and started walking toward the shimmering buildings. Megan craned her neck in order to view the tops. The massive columns of concrete, steel, and glass appeared to angle in at the top, as if squeezing out the sky. She bumped into a street lamp.

"Oops!" Mike slipped his arm into hers. "It looks like you need a little guidance." She was too awestruck to notice. Everything was so huge. "Up ahead on your left, is the New York Stock Exchange," Mike went on. "That's where the shaking happens." He and Megan walked casually along, arm in arm. Sara glanced over at the two and smirked. Megan chose to ignore her.

After a few minutes, Mike changed directions. "We're only a few streets over from the docks," he said. "If you'd like, we can take the ferry out to Ellis Island."

"And the Statue of Liberty?" Megan asked expectantly.

"Can't miss it," Mike answered. Crossing a busy street, he held Megan's hand tightly in his own, and never let go. As they neared the water, a brisk breeze swept in from the ocean, causing Megan to snuggle closer to Mike.

"Brrr," she shivered. "You're right, it's cold out here." Mike looked pleasantly surprised.

"Oh?" he smiled, putting his arm over Megan's shoulders. "I hadn't noticed." Sara rolled her eyes and groaned.

They turned a final corner revealing a sweeping view of the New York harbor. Magnificent ships steamed slowly through the choppy waters, a swirl of smaller craft darting in their wake. And in the distance, almost shrouded in fog, the majestic figure of the Statue of Liberty rose into the gray-blue sky. Megan stopped abruptly and caught her breath.

She had seen it on television, in history books, and on postcards. She'd even caught a glimpse of it from the window on the plane coming in. But now, seeing the monument rise before her into the mist, tears brimmed in her eyes. "Give me your tired, your poor, your huddled masses yearning to breathe free . . . "

" . . . the wretched refuse of your teeming shore—" Mike and Sara joined her. "Send these, the homeless, tempest tossed to me. I lift my lamp beside the golden door."

The blaring horn of the ferryboat broke the spell. "Come on." Mike grabbed Megan's hand and they all ran for the boat. Once on board, they found a spot along the railing where they could see the statue. The engines rumbled beneath their feet. Silently, they watched the lady grow larger and larger as they approached Liberty Island.

"Imagine what it must have been like arriving in America and seeing the statue for the first time." Sara drooped her elbows over the railing. "My grandpa was barely 16 when he emigrated to the United States, in 1906. He always talked about the 'Lady with the Lamp'."

"I didn't realize your folks were from Europe," Megan admitted.

Sara shrugged. "My mom and dad moved to Northern California when I was a baby, but my grandparents stayed in Brooklyn. My folks had my grandpa's name inscribed at Ellis Island. I hope I can find it."

Mike was surprised. "Really? My dad and his parents' names are there too. He was 5 years old when his parents came over—just after World War II."

"I guess I'm the only true American here, huh?" Megan teased. "Nothing glamorous in my past. My dad's parents decided to move to California from Oklahoma's dustbowl. Their car broke down in Albuquerque and the rest, as they say, is history." They all laughed.

The ferry docked and the three of them went ashore. They strolled about the island for more than an hour. Megan photographed the statue from every possible angle. They visited the gift shop at the base of the statue, inspecting the many curios carefully. At last, she chose a statue paperweight for her father and a commemorative spoon for Libby. Megan joined Sara at the cash register. "I guess I'm a typical tourist, huh?"

"Me too. See?" Sara held up a letter opener with the statue on the handle and an accordian of postcards. "For my dad," she explained.

Mike stood leaning against a wall near the exit. "Well, anybody game for a hike to the top?"

"Absolutely!" Megan cast him a mischievous glance. "Wanna' race?"

"I'll take you on anytime," Mike chuckled, leaning toward her.

"You two go ahead," Sara chimed in. "I climbed it a few weeks ago and believe me, once is enough. Besides, I want to look around the gift shop a little longer. Enjoy yourselves."

Megan shot Sara a withering look. Sara batted her eyes innocently, smiled sweetly, and turned into the store. Mike pulled at Megan's arm.

"There's an elevator to the top of the pedestal," he said, not noticing the exchange of looks. "We can walk on up from there." Megan followed Mike to the elevator.

Once again her skin felt clammy as the doors closed on the tiny space. *I can do this,* she told herself. *Like riding in a car, that's all.* Megan held her breath until the elevator came to a stop. When the elevator doors opened, she felt herself being swept along to the stone balcony by the crowd of chattering visitors. She looked out, 80 feet above the entrance and a little more than 150 feet above the misty gray sea below.

Two doorways led into the interior of the statue, one marked UP and one marked DOWN. Walking inside, Megan saw huge girders, twice as thick as a wrestler's body, reaching up as far as she could see. She remembered reading somewhere that the central iron cage had been designed and built by the man who erected the Eiffel Tower in Paris. Beyond the iron cage, she could see the Lady's copper skin, with its network of trusses and linkages, billowing like a huge metal tent. The lights cast distorted shadows on the deep folds of the copper skirt. Voices of those climbing the stairs bounced and echoed off the walls. It was like being inside a massive piece of machinery.

"Do you still want to race?" Mike was smiling at her from beside the first step in the long, winding stairway to the top.

She craned her neck and looked up.

"Uh, on second thought—" She laughed. "I'd rather not rush it." With a little bow, he stepped aside to let Megan go first. She started up the metal steps, counting as she went. The further up they climbed, the narrower the space became. At step number 75, they took a breather.

"Whew!" Megan puffed. "I can't imagine I was cold a few minutes ago." She brushed beads of perspiration from her forehead.

"This isn't nearly as bad as climbing the Washington Monument in D.C." Mike offered. "That thing will really take your breath away."

"Well, it's bad enough for me—especially the closeness." She stretched her arms out as if to push the walls back. "I never realized I had claustrophobia until I flew east."

Mike's brow wrinkled with concern, "I'm sorry. Why didn't you say something? We didn't have to climb the statue if you didn't want to."

She shook her head emphatically. "No, that's OK. I wouldn't have missed this for the world." After a few more minutes, they resumed the climb. *Eighty, ninety—we're a long way up. How high?* She tried to remember the statistics she'd read, but couldn't. She felt hot. The air was thick with humidity. She tugged at the neck of her sweater. *One-hundred and fifty, one-hundred and sixty . . .* All at once they were at the top. Stepping into the interior of the statue's head was like stepping inside the cranium of a giant. A spider-like cage supported the contours of the head. The crown, with the observation windows looking out at the harbor, wasn't much bigger than a small apartment kitchen. It was small. And stuffy.

But the view! Before them the gleaming skyline of New York spread out in a towering display. Megan was entranced.

As they peered out each window, Mike pointed out the various landmarks of the harbor and lower Manhattan. He moved in closer as he directed her attention to the different sights. But Megan inched away. Sensing her discomfort, Mike backed off. Which made her more uncomfortable still. She sighed.

How can I make it clear that I'm not ready for another relationship without feeling like such a heel? she wondered. *Why do things have to be so complicated?*

She dropped a quarter into one of the observation deck telescopes and stared out at the fog rolling in through the Narrows. She didn't hear him approach.

"So tell me about Alan." He acted nonchalant.

"Who?" Megan jerked around.

"Alan," Mike repeated. "When Sara first suggested you for the job, she doubted you'd come because Alan wouldn't like it. But you're here, so that makes me wonder what happened to Alan." He paused a moment. "I take it he's your boyfriend?" It was obvious the subject made him uncomfortable.

"Try fiancé," she retorted.

Mike gaped. "Fiancé! You're getting married?" He blushed bright

54

red and began to stammer. "Oh, I didn't know. I, uh, thought . . . well. Since you came I thought maybe . . . wow!" Mike ran his hand through his hair. "Congratulations." He looked like a wet puppy.

What a perfect opportunity! Megan thought. *If Mike thinks I'm still engaged, then he'd respect that and leave me alone. Then I wouldn't feel so guilty putting him off all the time. Yet,* she sighed, *I can't lie to him. That's what Alan did to me. Lying only makes things worse.* She turned back to the telescope.

"Actually, Alan and I *were* engaged," Megan said at last. "We broke up."

"Oh, sorry." Relief flooded his eyes. Then he caught himself. "I didn't mean to pry."

"It's over and done now." Her voice choked in her throat. "Almost, anyway."

Mike turned and stared out at the harbor for a few minutes before speaking. "Give yourself time, you'll heal."

Her eyes flashed with sudden fury. "What do you know about it!" Mike was startled. She waved a finger in his face. "Dumping girls is a favorite male sport, isn't it? Well I for one have had it. Never again!" Megan's voice echoed off the metal walls. Mike flinched. The other visitors turned to look. Surprised at her own outburst, Megan stared fixedly out the nearest window.

For what seemed like an eternity no one said anything. Finally, Mike spoke up.

"We ought to head back down," he said softly. "Sara's probably waiting."

"I'm sorry, I didn't mean . . ." Megan began.

"You don't need to explain," Mike smiled. "I'm the one who should be apologizing. You're still really feeling it, and I'm coming on to you all the time like some kind of insensitive jerk. I'm sorry." He led her toward the stairs. "From now on I'll try to do better, OK?" They headed down the stairs.

When they reached the bottom, Sara waved to them from the dock. "Hurry!" she called. "The ferry is leaving for Ellis Island." Mike grabbed Megan's hand and set off down the walkway. They boarded the ferry just as the boatman was lifting the ramp.

Ellis Island was an imposing sight. Clusters of restored buildings vied for attention along the paved walkways. At the visitor's center a dramatic exhibit recorded the names of immigrants who passed through on the way to their promised land. With the help of a directory,

Sara found her grandfather's name. She ran her fingers across the carved surface and wept. No one noticed, since others around her were doing the same thing.

Mike showed them his family's names. "They escaped from Austria to England just before the war. After the Armistice, they came to America."

History had never seemed so real to Megan before. More than dates and battles and bloodshed, it was real people searching for new beginnings, much like herself.

An hour later they were back at the dock walking up to Mike's car. "How about a quick tour of the Empire State Building?" he asked. "The view is incredible, even after dark."

"Do we have to walk up?" Megan joked.

"You might want to," Sara laughed. "The elevators can put your stomach on the ceiling." Megan turned pale.

"I can hardly wait."

Due to the light Sunday afternoon traffic, they reached midtown in record time. Inside the Empire State Building, they paused for the elevator.

"Ah, now this is the way I prefer to climb 102 stories," Sara said as she stepped inside.

Oh help! Megan thought. *What am I doing here?* She closed her eyes as the elevator doors slid shut. Beads of sweat formed on her forehead. She felt perspiration trickle down her spine. Her stomach lurched as the elevator began its ascent.

"Are you going to be all right?" Mike whispered, slipping his arm about her shoulders.

"Yes-yes, I'll-I'll be f-f-fine," Megan stammered, her breath coming in shallow gasps. When the elevator stopped on the eighty-sixth floor, her stomach continued on without her. At last the doors slid open. Megan rushed into the marble-lined waiting area. Mike and Sara hurried after her.

"Are you OK?" Sara asked.

"I don't know." Megan was breathless. "I just realized that I still have to go back down in that thing!"

"We're not at the top yet," Mike warned. "We have to take a second elevator the rest of the way up."

"What!" Megan stared in horror. Mike and Sara looked at her worriedly. She gritted her teeth. "Let's get it over with." They headed toward the second elevator.

"Are you sure you want to go through with this?" Mike asked.

"Don't start giving me options or we'll never make it to the top," Megan responded. The doors of the elevator closed behind them.

At last they reached the observation deck.

One look at the gigantic city spread out beneath her, and Megan forgot all her discomfort on the way up. "This is the most spectacular thing I've ever seen," she gushed. Mike guided her to the railing. He pointed out the aluminum spired Chrysler Building as well as Central Park. Far below, thousands of people coursed through the streets, looking like tiny specks of color swirling about.

"So many people living in one small area," she said. "How will they all ever learn about Jesus?"

Mike chuckled. "The thought of evangelizing New York has always been *the* challenge for me. For a lot of others, too."

"Is that why you came here?"

"Partly." His face turned sober. "I always imagined that God wanted me to work with inner-city kids. But after being here, seeing the problems, getting a feel of the ministry, I'm not so sure." He leaned back against the wrought iron fencing.

"Why?"

"I can't explain it." He paused. "It's like trying on a new pair of blue jeans—not quite the right fit."

A rueful smile crossed Megan's face. "I think I know what you mean. Up until a few weeks ago, my future seemed pretty certain. A white satin wedding gown. Alan. And a honeymoon cruise to Mazatlan. Now . . ." Her words drifted off into the late afternoon breeze.

"If it's any comfort, we can be confident that God is leading in our lives." Mike looked out over the city. "He promises to always be with us, to the far corners of the earth. What more can we ask?"

"Please, Mike, no clichés," Megan grimaced and walked away. "I've heard and endured them all."

Mike stared after her. "Promises, Megan, not clichés."

She shrugged and walked into the building.

Megan taped the last of the construction paper cutouts to the bulletin board. The Thanksgiving scene the children were making was a riot of different colors and styles. *Just like the children,* Megan thought to herself.

She glanced at the clock on the wall. *Six-thirty! I'd better hurry if I want be back at Mama Grace's for supper,* she told herself. *Maybe I'll just grab a bagel and a carton of orange juice at the corner deli on the way home. There's so much to do before I leave for the airport in the morning.* She smiled at the thought of being home again. She pictured herself riding her horse, Amby, out across the mesa, celebrating Thanksgiving Day with her father, and participating in her dad and Libby's wedding.

Though it never totally disappeared, Megan's homesickness had lightened considerably since coming to New York. And like it or not, it was mostly because of Mike. No matter what she did, the man refused to be put off. Such persistence was hard to ignore.

Though she was still confused about her feelings for Mike, other questions had cleared. Teaching was a joy. Her students were a continual blessing to her spirits. She now felt certain that God was opening a new door for her in teaching. All she needed now was to complete her elementary education requirements. After that, perhaps she would begin working on a Masters degree in education.

She filled her time with school activities during the day and grading papers in the evening. And on the weekends, Mike got her and Sara involved in youth activities at the church: Sabbath visits to nursing homes, a church service along the Jersey shore, a trip to the New York Aquarium, an autumn excursion to the Berkshires.

One evening on the way home from school, Mike had suggested going to Coney Island for the "best" roasted corn-on-the-cob in the city.

Megan's eyes lit up. "Hey, that sounds like fun. I'll see if Sara wants to go." Mike cleared his throat. "Uh, I wasn't inviting Sara this time. I thought that maybe just you and I could . . . um . . ."

Megan fell silent. Inside, a tug of war broke out between her desire to go with Mike, and her fear of going without Sara. "Oh . . . well, I guess . . . "

"Great!" Mike cut in. "I'll pick you up around 5:30. Wear something comfortable, especially your shoes. We'll be walking a lot." His eyes were bright. "I want to introduce you to the Cyclone. It's the scariest roller coaster ride you've ever seen."

"I'm thrilled," Megan grimaced.

When she told her roommate, Sara grinned with delight. "You can borrow my cream cable-knit sweater if you like. It can be chilly along the boardwalk at this time of year."

"Sara! Don't make more of this than it really is."

"Who's making more of it? It's just a date, right?" Sara smirked.

"Right! So wipe that smug expression off your face," Megan sputtered as she pulled the heavy wool sweater down over her head.

"Tsk! Tsk!" Sara clucked. "As the Bard once said, 'The lady doth protest too much.'" Megan picked up one of her bedroom slippers and threw it at her. Sara ducked and laughed.

Megan heard Mike's car pull up out front. Rather than risk having Sara or any other member of the family say something embarassing, Megan raced down the stairs and out the door.

"Oomph!" She slammed directly into Mike, coming through the door.

"Good evening to you too," he said, steadying her. "Are you all right?"

"Fine!" She pasted on her brightest smile. "Didn't want to keep you waiting." Glancing over her shoulder, she grabbed his arm and propelled him back down the porch steps. "Let's get out of here."

Coney Island was a tumult of color and light. The Cyclone turned out to be everything Mike had promised. As the car plunged down the first hill, Megan screamed until her throat hurt. Lurching to a stop at the gangway, her eyes glistened with excitement. Mike helped her out of the car. "That was great!" she bubbled. "That was really great!"

"Want to go again?"

"Not a chance."

He laughed, took her hand and led her down the ramp to the sidewalk. "The roasted corn is over this way."

Steam billowed from the crowded concession stands along the sidewalk. He payed for two piping hot cobs of corn and handed her one. Melted butter dripped down her fingers as she bit into the succulent kernels. "Ummm." Her face lighted up. "This is delicious, Mike!" she said between bites. "Really delicious!"

"Here . . ." He dabbed a stray kernel from her cheek with his napkin. He studied her face for a moment, then turned back to the counter. "Needs more salt," he said. Megan watched the strange conglomeration of people milling about the boardwalk. Men in Italian silk suits and sporting Rolex watches mixed with street people dressed in shabby rags. Orange, purple, and pink-haired teens shared counter space with snowy-haired grandmothers and their bowler-hatted escorts. Megan saw a black limousine pull up to the curb behind them. A uniformed chauffeur got out, purchased an order of hot dogs and corn, and walked back to the car. A few words at the rear window and the food disappeared inside. *So much for rubbing shoulders with the common people,* Megan thought to herself. *It must be like living in a cocoon.* The car disappeared in the traffic.

"I can't believe so many people are here at this time of year," she said.

Mike chuckled and took another bite of corn. "You can come here on the coldest day in January and find a crowd. Would you like another piece of corn, or maybe a soda or something?"

She shook her head and dabbed her fingers onto a paper napkin. "Thanks, but I've had plenty."

They strolled past boarded up stalls, past the kiddie rides, past the occasional hawker, down between the wooden girders supporting the boardwalk and out onto the open beach. The sun hovered blood-red just over the horizon, spilling a fiery glow on the water. Megan walked across the loose sand toward the pounding surf. The boisterous sounds of the carnival behind her faded into the distance.

"Don't you love the ocean?" she said, taking a deep breath of the salty air. "It always makes me feel so alive!" She whirled in circles with childlike abandon, her arms stretched toward the sky. She dropped cross-legged onto the sand, humming a cherished hymn. "I sing the mighty power of God that made the oceans rise . . ."

Mike sat down beside her. "That's a favorite of mine, too," he said. "You can really sense the spirit of it out here." They listened to the roar of the ocean until a ceiling of stars dotted an indigo sky.

"I always feel so close to God by the ocean. Alan and I used to . . ." Megan hesitated. "Mike, I've got to be fair with you." She ran handfuls of sand through her fingers. "I think of you as a great friend. You've become almost like a brother to me."

"A brother!" Mike exclaimed.

"Mike, try to understand," Megan pleaded. "I don't think I can deal with the idea of starting a new relationship, even with you." She looked back at the ocean. "I need some time, that's all."

"All right, Megan," Mike said. "You've been honest with me. Now I should be honest with you." He turned to face her. "You've become too special to me to risk losing you, so I will play by your rules. But, understand, I have no intentions of backing off from our friendship."

Her eyes widened in surprise. "Oh, I wouldn't want you to. I love . . . I mean, I enjoy being with you." She felt her face redden. "If I had a brother, I would want him to be just like you."

Mike rose to his feet and extended his hands to help her up. One tug and she found herself inches from his face. "If the rules change, be sure to let me know, OK?"

She didn't answer. Nor did she object when they strolled hand in hand back to the park and on to the subway station.

During the weeks that followed, Megan relaxed and enjoyed her time with Mike. Now that the terms of their relationship were clearly defined, she no longer felt the need to protest Sara's matchmaking attempts. She especially enjoyed the long talks she and Mike had in Mama Grace's kitchen on Saturday nights after everyone else had gone to bed. They related childhood antics. They discussed their views on raising children and their beliefs on the secrets of a happy marriage. They debated the finer points of theology and shared their dreams of what they hoped heaven would be like. When Mike left for a ministers' retreat in Massachusetts, she missed him.

With the last of the Thanksgiving decorations mounted on the classroom walls, Megan's work preparing for the holidays was nearly done. A substitute teacher would be filling in for her while she was in New Mexico for Thanksgiving and her father's wedding. Turning out the lights, she headed down the corridor. This was one of the weeknights Mama Grace and Sara volunteered their time at the community center. Alvin would be looking after the other children until Megan arrived. She stepped up her pace. The thought of Alvin alone, struggling with a houseful of energetic kids, made her chuckle. She didn't want to leave him alone any longer than necessary.

Megan need not have worried. When she reached the house, the kitchen had been cleaned, the younger children had taken their showers, and Alvin was reading them a story.

"I'm sorry I'm late, Alvin," she apologized. "I had a lot of turkeys to deal with."

"Piece of cake," he smiled. "It wasn't hard. The kids knew what to do." After kissing each of them goodnight, she hurried upstairs to her room to pack. When Sara tiptoed in later that evening, she was in bed and asleep.

The next morning, Mike drove her to the airport. She insisted he drop her at the terminal rather than pay to park his car. Reluctantly, he agreed. Checking her bags with a porter, he led her to a quiet spot away from the crowded sidewalk. After a simple prayer for her safe travel, he squeezed her hands. "You be careful," he whispered, "and hurry back, ya' hear?"

Before she realized what she was saying, she responded, "I'll miss you."

"Do you mean that?" He looked deep into her eyes. She nodded. He covered her hands with his. "When you return next week, I'd like to explore that thought a little further if you don't mind. But for now, you have a plane . . ."

"Hey, move this heap of junk, will ya!" A harsh voice from behind them broke the spell of the moment. An airport security officer tapped the faded hood of Mike's Toyota. "You can't park here, it's a loading zone. Can't you read?"

"Guess I'd better go," he said. "Here." He planted a kiss on her left cheek and ran to his car. "Something to think about."

"That was a brotherly thing to do," Megan teased.

He bowed with the flourish of a cavalier poet. "My thoughts exactly, madam." He hopped into his car and drove away.

Thanksgiving week flew by in a whirlwind of wedding preparations. Even though the wedding would be held at Libby's church in Tucumkari, Megan still had a lot to do to get ready. She scrubbed the ranch house from one end to the other. "I won't have Libby returning from her honeymoon to a dirty house!" she told her father.

Megan treasured those moments she spent with her father that week. Libby and Herb had decided to spend the holidays with their respective families, so Megan had her father all to herself. They took walks to the overlook, went shopping together, and ate out. On their tour of Old Town, she bought Mike a silver and turquoise bolo tie.

"He'll love it," she laughed. "But I know he'll never wear it. He's too much the city boy."

Herb chuckled. "Coming from the right person, I suspect he might."

On Thanksgiving morning, Megan awakened early to begin the holiday preparations. She stood at the kitchen counter rolling out pie-crust dough when the telephone rang. Her father was across the room, making a pot of oatmeal for breakfast. "Can you get that, Daddy? My hands are coated with flour."

"Sure." He set the pot on a hot pad and ran for the phone.

She filled the two pie shells with pumpkin filling and placed them in the hot oven. She'd begun rolling out the remaining dough into bread-sticks when her father ambled into the kitchen. "He seems like a really nice guy, Meggy darling."

"Who is, Daddy?" She drew a sharp kitchen knife through the dough.

Her father sputtered. "The guy you've been talking about nonstop since you got home and the guy I have been talking with on the telephone for the last 15 minutes, that's who."

She whirled around. "Mike? On the phone? Why didn't you tell me? Where was he calling from?"

He scooped out a serving of oatmeal and dumped it into a bowl. "He *was* on the phone. I told him you were in the middle of rolling out pie-dough, so he said he'd call back later."

"Oh." Megan turned back to the counter, trying to hide her disappointment. Herb sprinkled some brown sugar on the steaming cereal and sat down at the table.

"He was calling from his parent's home in a town called Glens Falls, I believe. Is that anywhere near where you live?"

"No, Glens Falls is about 200 miles north of the city." She rinsed her hands at the sink. "Uh, did he say when he'd call back?"

"This evening around 8:00, our time, if he can get through. If not, he sends his love and he'll see you when you get back to New York." Herb glanced at his daughter out of the corner of his eye. "So, when will I get to meet this Michael Feldman?"

Drying her hands on a tea towel, Megan tried to act casual. "Oh, Daddy! It's no big deal. We're friends—that's all."

"If you say so, Meggy." He dug into his bowl of oatmeal.

Megan waited all evening, but Mike's call never came. Around 9:00

she tried to call him, but all the long distance lines were busy. Finally she gave up and went to bed.

On Friday morning, she and her father drove to Tucumkari. Libby's family was in a mad rush making all the final preparations for the wedding on Saturday evening, and Herb and Megan waded right in to help. They had a full day of errands and last minute decisions, ending with a rehearsal at the church that afternoon. Later, the families gathered at Libby's oldest daughter's home for supper and evening worship.

For some reason everything she said or did that evening reminded her somehow of Mike. When Libby led them in a medley of favorite hymns around the piano, she remembered the deserted Coney Island beach. "I sing the mighty power of God that made the oceans rise . . . " When everyone knelt to pray, she remembered Mike's prayer at the airport. When her father kissed Libby goodnight, Megan caressed her own cheek, feeling Mike's soft goodbye kiss. *What is wrong with me?* she wondered.

After lunch the next day, Libby's daughter insisted that her mother take a short nap. So Megan and her father decided to drive out to Conchas Lake. It felt good to escape the confining quarters of the crowded house. They parked the truck and followed a hiking trail up to the top of a ridge.

They perched on a giant boulder and stared out across the valley below. "How are you feeling about Alan lately?" her father asked.

She inhaled the clean, dry, desert air. "This is going to sound strange, but at times, I can hardly remember what he looks like."

"That's good. I wasn't too keen on that young man anyway," her father admitted.

She grinned, snatched his hat off his head and put it on hers. "I kind of figured that out. You've never been too subtle, you know."

He yanked a stalk of prairie grass free and stuck the end of it in his mouth. "So tell me more about this Mike character."

She tilted her head to one side and squinted up at him. "I'm not sure there's much left to tell. Like you said, I've been talking about him the entire week." She rolled the sandy soil between her fingers. "He really cares about people. I don't think there's a selfish bone in his body."

"You like him a lot, don't you?" Herb asked. Megan sighed.

"Yeah, I do." She looked across the rocky landscape. "But I don't think I'm ready for another relationship. After what happened with Alan I feel . . . drained."

"I know, honey." Herb put a reassuring arm around her shoulders. "But sometimes you have to move on to get away from the past. If this Mike fella is worth having, I wouldn't let Alan reach in and spoil it for you. He's done enough. You make the decisions now."

Megan nodded. They talked until the sun neared the horizon, then hiked back down the trail to the truck and drove back to town. By the time they reached home, got cleaned up and dressed for the wedding, it was well past dark.

When they reached the church, the place was buzzing with life. From the moment they stepped into the building, they were caught up in the activity. The best man grabbed her father and ushered him off. One of Libby's daughters whisked Megan away to the ladies' dressing area. There was Libby, radiant in her candlelight lace dress. Megan's eyes misted with tears as she hurried to Libby's side and kissed her cheek. "Welcome to the family, Mom." Libby beamed.

"Thank you, my daughter."

During the next hour, the wedding party was herded from one place to another by the photographer and his take-charge assistant. When the first guests started arriving, everyone was hustled out of view.

Waiting for the wedding to begin, Megan thumbed through the program. On the cover in bright golden letters were the words: "Delight yourself in the Lord and He will give you the desires of your heart" Psalm 37:4. The text blurred before her eyes. Mike had quoted that phrase to her many times.

Megan finally admitted to herself that God really was giving her the desire of her heart. She wanted a loving home and a Christian husband with whom to share it. God knew all along that Alan—poor, confused Alan—couldn't give her that. She shuddered as she pictured what might have been. She bowed her head and whispered a heartfelt prayer of gratitude.

Once set in motion, the wedding progressed on its own. The procession, the sermon, the recessional, the receiving line. Before Megan realized it, her father was taking her aside at the reception and kissing her goodbye.

"Be careful, Meggy darlin'," he said, his eyes filled with love and concern. "Take your time with this guy." Herb stroked her hair. "Did I tell you how much I enjoyed the week we had together? It will always be special to me."

Megan choked back her tears. "I love you, Daddy. I know you and

Libby will be very happy together." He gave her a hug and stepped back to Libby's side. After running the gauntlet of rice, he and Libby climbed into the car to leave. As he helped his bride into the car, Herb turned and blew a kiss to Megan. Then they were gone.

The next morning she drove back to the ranch. She gave the house a quick cleaning, then packed for her return to New York. At the airport, she parked her dad's truck in the long term parking lot. Herb was to pick it up on his return. Collecting her bags, she walked to the terminal.

Merry Christmas! A gold and red banner spread across the main entrance. In the few days since she had arrived, Christmas decorations had sprung up everywhere. Her spirits rose at the sight of the huge glittering wreaths and brightly colored ribbons. She loved the giant evergreens covered with miniature lights and handmade Native American decorations. *How different Christmas will be this year,* she thought. *Instead of touring Albuquerque's "Old Town" on Christmas Eve, I'll be singing carols with Mama Grace and the children.*

She hurried to the airline ticket counter and checked in her luggage. Pulling the strap of her carry-on case over her shoulder, she rushed down the corridors to her gate of departure.

"American Airlines flight #1207 is now boarding for St. Louis, New York, Boston . . ." As the first words blared over the intercom Megan dashed for the gate, impatient to be on her way. This time, as she quickly boarded and found a seat, Megan was unaware of the crowd jostling around her.

As the plane lifted off the runway Megan leaned back in her seat. This trip East marked a new beginning for her. During the time at home she had finally realized that her love for Alan was dead and gone. And while she might not actually be in love with Mike, she was certainly very fond of him.

She thought of her father. She remembered the pain he endured during her mother's long illness. And after her death, he had been so very lonely. Yet whenever Megan asked about it, he'd quoted the text, "I will never leave you, nor forsake you." Herb believed every word. "Standing on God's promises, Meggy," he would say. "They help me make it through each day." Then she remembered the happiness on Herb's face when Libby arrived. Megan could see her father had been right all along. "Thank You, God" she prayed softly. "Thank You for Libby."

The plane droned on, high above the clouds. *Will this flight never end?* Megan wondered. She tried to sleep; she tried to read. Yet the time still dragged. *I wish Mike were here,* she thought. *I have so much to tell him.* Megan sighed. How many times during the past week had she caught herself wishing that? Like it or not Mike was a major player in her life right now. Unfortunately, at that moment he was driving down from Glens Falls. Sara would pick her up at the airport, not Mike. She wouldn't see him until morning.

When Megan got off the plane, Sara was waiting. As they headed down the crowded concourse, Sara relished every detail of Megan's trip and the wedding.

"I get to travel next time," said Sara. "Mom and Dad called on Thanksgiving Day. They bought me a ticket home for my Christmas present. Isn't that teriffic?"

"Lucky you!" Megan smiled. "It'll do you good to get out of the rush of the city for a while. You'll have a blast."

As they emerged from the terminal, a frigid blast of wind swept over them. Megan gasped. "Oooh!" She huddled inside her heavy coat. "I forgot how cold it could get here."

"Welcome to the Northeast," Sara laughed. They dashed across the open-air causeway leading to the parking garage. When they finally reached the car, Megan's teeth were chattering and her fingers tingled from the cold.

"Brrr!" Megan snuggled down in the seat. "Is it always this cold in New York?"

"The weather report says we're getting arctic air sweeping down from Canada," Sara said. "But who cares? It's Christmas!"

Megan was just beginning to feel warm again as Sara pulled off the freeway onto the city streets. Multicolored lights twinkled in store fronts; garlands of silver and green draped across the busy streets. Candy canes, Santas, and reindeer pulling sleighs decked the street lamps. Everywhere Megan looked she saw symbols of Christmas. Even the row houses no longer faded into a drab sameness. Bright colors and festive decorations revealed the individuality of their owners, hidden the rest of the year.

As the car stopped in front of Mama Grace's, the front door burst open. Excited children poured out of the house and down the steps to the car.

"You're back, Miss Megan. You're back," chimed little Joelle, who was the first to reach the car.

"I didn't like the substitute teacher," said the second-grader Tanya, opening Megan's door. "She didn't smile. I missed you."

"I missed you too." Megan hugged the girl and stepped out of the car.

"I'll carry your suitcases up to your room," said Alvin as he took the keys from Sara and opened the trunk.

"You kids are going to catch your death of colds if you don't get in here right away," Mama Grace scolded from the porch. "Good to have you back Megan. Got some hot cocoa ready and waiting."

Megan paused at the curb. She was absorbed by the familiar scene. Her eyes twinkled with happiness. "It feels good to be back, Mama," said Megan as she climbed the steps.

Mama Grace wrapped an arm about her shoulder and drew her into the house. "So how was the wedding? I want to hear every detail."

The family gathered around the gray formica kitchen table and swapped stories about the previous week. As usual, everyone was enjoying themselves so much no one noticed the time.

Suddenly, Mama Grace glanced at the kitchen clock. "Why it's nearly 11:00!" She hustled the children toward the stairs. "C'mon, off to bed with you. There's school tomorrow, you know."

The children groaned but obeyed. Tanya gave Megan one last hug before following the other children up the stairs. "I like you lots, Miss Megan," she whispered.

"I like you lots too," Megan smiled.

"You two get to bed too," Mama Grace said to Megan and Sara, still sitting at the table. "It won't do to have grownups setting a bad example."

Laughing, Megan and Sara hurried to their room. While Sara took a shower, Megan started unpacking her bags. She had just put the last of her jeans in the drawer when the front doorbell rang. The sound of a familiar male voice caught her attention.

"Anybody home?" It was Mike. She could hear Mama Grace bustling down the stairs to meet him.

"Shush now!" Mama Grace chided, barely concealing a good-natured chuckle in her voice. "What kind of man comes stalking around this time of night? You should be ashamed."

"I'm glad to see you, too," Mike deadpanned. "I was hoping Megan was still up."

"And here I thought you came for me," Mama Grace retorted.

"Well, Megan's already asleep, poor child. Traveling all that way . . ."

Megan dashed across the room and flung the bedroom door open. "Mama Grace," she called, leaning over the mahogany railing. Mike and Mama Grace stared up at her from the doorway. Suddenly she paused. What could she say?

"Oh, hi Mike." She pretended to be surprised.

"You're supposed to be in bed," Mama Grace said sternly.

"Hi, Megan," Mike answered. "How was New Mexico?"

"Great! I've got lots to tell you."

"In the morning, child," Mama Grace protested.

"Oh, Mama," Megan smiled. "It'll only take a minute. Just let me change and I'll be right down." She hurried into her room and began rifling through the dresser.

"Slow down!" Sara quipped from her bed. "You'd think you're eager to see him or something." Megan blushed. She pulled on a pair of jeans and a sweatshirt.

"I'm just glad to see a good friend, that's all," Megan responded, running a brush through her hair.

"Good *friend?* Yeah, right," said Sara as she rolled her eyes. Ignoring her, Megan dashed down the stairs.

At the landing, she paused to compose herself. *It wouldn't do to trip on the first step and fall head over heels at his feet,* she decided. She took a deep breath and slowly descended the last few steps to the entryway.

Mike was waiting.

"Hi," he whispered. "Sorry about showing up so late. I just got in from Glens Falls and I just couldn't wait to see you."

"I'm glad you came by," she said with a goofy smile. "So how was your Thanksgiving?"

"Great," he beamed. For a moment there was an awkward silence between them. Megan decided he looked as silly as she did. Mike plowed ahead. "So have you heard from your dad and his new bride?"

"Of course not! They're on their honeymoon." She led him into the parlor. The soft light of a single table lamp cast a warm glow over the well-worn furnishings. They sat down on an overstuffed sofa and began talking about their vacations. She told him about the special week she and her dad had enjoyed.

"Your father sounds like a really thoughtful guy," Mike said. "We had a nice talk."

"You'd like him. He's terrific." She stared down at her hands and chipped away at the imaginary imperfections on her fingernails. "I

69

know all daughters say that about their fathers, but in my case, it's true." Out of the corner of her eye, she glimpsed a grin on Mike's face.

"Don't laugh! He *is* a great guy." She playfully punched his shoulder.

Mike raised his hands defensively, "I believe you, I believe you." Megan smiled and went on.

"Dad has a perpetual gleam of laughter in his eyes. Even when he's serious, it's there—right below the surface."

"And, I'll bet you are the apple of his eye." Mike grinned the lopsided grin she liked so much.

"You could say that," she admitted. "But I bet it's the same with your parents."

"Oh, speaking of my folks, I almost forgot. I've been instructed to give you this." He reached in his jacket pocket and pulled out an envelope. "It's from my mom."

She opened the envelope and read the letter. "It's an invitation to spend Christmas vacation with your family in Glens Falls."

"I know," Mike admitted. "I planned to just ask you, but she insisted on sending a formal invitation. She has this thing about doing things 'the right way,' as she puts it."

"I agree with her," Megan said as she reread the letter.

"You two are going to really hit it off." Mike rose nervously to his feet. "You will come, won't you? Don't worry. I explained to her that we were just friends, almost like brother and sister, in fact."

She stood up and put the letter back into the envelope. "Almost. But not quite."

"I beg your pardon?" Mike's easygoing smile shifted into a look of intense interest. He bent low to peer into her eyes. "Could you clarify that statement please?"

Suddenly, the gong of the dining room clock rang out. Megan began fussing with her watch. "Boy, it's getting late! And I'm sure to have a massive case of jet lag. Guess it's time to go, huh?" She leaped toward the doorway like a frightened fawn.

Mike never took his eyes off her. He backed warily out the door onto the porch. Their eyes met. "See you tomorrow then."

"Goodnight." Megan closed the door. Mike's footsteps retreated into the night. Megan pounded her forehead against the door jamb. "What a wimp! I had my chance and blew it!"

CHAPTER

7

The huge Christmas tree loomed high above the swirling skaters at Rockefeller Center. Its long evergreen branches were decked with thousands of twinkling lights and strung with garlands of silver and gold. Christmas carols filled the evening air. The noise of the city seemed a thousand miles away.

Mike rented a pair of skates for each of them. They found a bench alongside the rink and sat down. He quickly laced his skates, then knelt down on the ice to help Megan. She eyed the silver blades warily. "I don't think I can do this, Mike."

"Aw, there's nothing to it." He slid the skate onto her foot and began tightening the laces. "I think I was skating before I could walk. I was playing ice hockey when I was 9 years old."

"Big expert, huh?" she groused. "Can't wait to get you on one of my dad's Appaloosas."

"Touché," laughed Mike. He finished tying the laces and sat down beside her to put on his own skates. When he finished he stood up and held out his arms. "Here, give me your hands and I'll help you get started." Megan struggled to her feet. She stood helplessly, clinging to Mike's arm. He smiled. "That's not so bad, is it?"

"Now I know how a new born colt feels," Megan said, her ankles wobbling beneath her.

"Just bend your knees a little," he coaxed. "That's right. You're getting the idea." Before she could protest, Megan found herself skimming across the ice beside Mike. "See? I told you it was easy."

Megan only glared. She was much too busy concentrating on her feet. It seemed they insisted on wandering off independent of her and of one another.

"Keep your skates together," he advised. "And pointing straight ahead. That is, if you can."

"Cute, Mike!"

Around and around they skated. The brisk winter breeze stung Megan's cheeks and tousled her hair. While she wasn't ready to admit it to Mike yet, this skating idea was almost fun. After a few times around the rink, Mike drew her closer to his side. Megan snuggled securely into the hollow of his arm and allowed him to guide her across the ice.

Suddenly two boys whistled by them. Engrossed in their game of tag, the boys zipped between the other skaters. The leader swept by so closely that Mike swerved to avoid a collision, only to clip the skate of the second boy as he darted by on the other side. Mike's feet crossed up, spilling them both flat on the ice.

"What kind of fancy footwork was that?" Megan laughed at the startled, bemused look on Mike's face. She could hear the spectators alongside the rink laughing too.

"Are you all right?" He helped her to her feet and brushed ice shavings from her jacket. "Would you like to take a break for a few minutes?"

"At a table, preferrably," she answered, moving unsteadily toward the side of the rink. They sat down at one of the small tables along the edge of the ice. From there, they talked and watched as other hapless skaters lurched by. Mike kept looking at her carefully. "Are you sure you're all right?"

"Of course I am," Megan laughed. "I'm not a china doll, you know. I don't break that easily."

"I just don't want to take any chances. That was a pretty hard fall you took."

"With your help, I might add."

"Don't remind me," Mike laughed.

How different from Alan, she thought. Alan would have been all-consumed with his own bruised dignity, worried about how foolish she had made him look in front of all those people. But Mike laughed along with everyone else. To him, it was fun. *How could I have been so blind?* she thought.

The weeks before Christmas swirled by in a flurry of holiday activities. A sudden cold snap brought with it a blanket of snow that covered the gray asphalt of the city. The couple made the most of it by taking long walks, sledding in Central Park, and touring the animated

Christmas display at the giant A&S department store. And Megan was certain they'd sampled pizza from every shop in the city.

Mike organized the youth from his church into a caroling group to sing in the neighborhood. On Saturday and Sunday evenings, Sara led the small choir of singers, while Mike and Megan distributed literature and visited with people in their homes.

Between houses, Mike also managed to rifle a snowball or two in Megan's direction—a challenge she couldn't ignore. They would run laughing and shouting across the slippery sidewalks, much to the amusement of Sara and the kids.

One couple they visited especially impressed Megan. John and Frieda Knapp had to be near 80 years old. John was so crippled with arthritis he could hardly open the door. Yet he and Frieda insisted on inviting the entire group into their home for hot cider and cookies. During the short visit, Megan found herself charmed by the tenderness John showed Frieda and the obvious love and respect Frieda displayed toward John. *How can two people can stay in love so long?* she wondered.

All too quickly their visit was over. Promising to return soon, Mike and Megan bid the kind old couple goodnight and led the group back to the church. Later that evening on their way home, Mike suggested he and Megan drive to the Varrazano-Narrows Bridge for a late night view of the city lights.

"Didn't you just love Mr. and Mrs. Knapp?" Megan snuggled into her seat. "They seemed like such nice people—so much in love with one another. Frieda—she insisted I call her by her first name—said they would be celebrating their sixtieth wedding anniversary on Christmas Day. Can you imagine?"

"John invited us back for Bible studies," Mike said. "I scheduled the first one for Tuesday night. Would you like to go with me?"

"Oh, yes." Megan's eyes danced with eagerness.

Mike found a turnout along the parkway and stopped the car. White lights, like a giant strand of pearls outlined the graceful cables spanning the Narrows. Lights danced on the surface of the water. They watched for a while, making small talk. But Megan felt no real need for conversation. She felt secure, happy, and at peace. *Thank you, God,* she prayed silently. *Thank you for Mike.*

It was after midnight before Mike suggested they return home. Throughout the short ride back to Mama Grace's, Megan's heart raced in anticipation. *It's now or never!* she told herself. *Do it!* When the car stopped she leaped out before Mike could turn off the engine.

"Hey!" Mike called out. "Where are you going?" Megan leaned back in the open car door.

"Just thought you'd like to know, well, I've been doing a lot of praying about it and for me, at least, the rules have definitely changed. G'night." She slammed the door, whirled about, and dashed up the steps into the house.

"Goodnight?" He lunged across to the passenger side of the car. "What? Megan, wait!" But she was gone.

Mike called early the next morning.

"What kind of stunt was that you pulled last night?" he kidded.

"Stunt?" asked Megan innocently. "Why, I merely wanted to inform you of a change in the rules. You said you wanted to know. So now you know."

"We need to talk," he answered. "How about taking a ride on the Staten Island Ferry? I can be there in 10 minutes."

"Make it 20 and you've got a deal," Megan responded happily. "See you then."

They drove to Staten Island and boarded the ferryboat for Manhattan. Finding a quiet spot along the brass railing, they talked.

"When did you first realize you cared for me, as more than a brother, that is?" Mike adjusted the heavy wool scarf about Megan's neck and lifted her coat collar up about her face.

"I never really thought of you as a brother." She raised her eyes to meet his. "I only said that because I was scared. It seemed like the safest thing to say."

"Well, you were right. A brother!"

She leaned out over the brass rail to watch the gray-green water tumble by the side of the boat. "When I was in New Mexico, I took a serious look at you and at me. I tried to tell you that night in the parlor."

"I thought so. At least I wanted to believe that's what you started to say," Mike said. "This may sound corny, but you did strange things to my heart when you flashed those steely gray eyes at me in the airport that first day, remember?" He laughed. "And then the Hershey kisses—that did it."

Megan smiled. She watched the waves lapping against the bow. "You were right, you know—about God never leaving us to stumble on alone," she said thoughtfully. "All along, God knew that my goals and Alan's goals didn't mesh and would only bring us both pain."

Mike flinched at the mention of Alan's name. Instinctively, she placed her hand on his arm and moved closer. "Right when I thought I could never care for anyone ever again, God introduced me to a persistent young preacher who steamrolled over every one of my carefully built defenses."

"I almost gave up a time or two," he admitted.

"I'm glad you didn't."

That night Megan wrote to Mike's mother, accepting her invitation for Christmas.

The day school let out for Christmas break, Megan felt as restless as her students. Even a classroom Christmas party couldn't make the time go by fast enough. After she dismissed the children at noon, she quickly cleaned the room and washed the boards. She had just removed the last Christmas decoration from the wall when Mike's face appeared around the edge of the classroom door.

"Ready?" he asked, his face beaming.

"In a minute." Megan tugged at an overstuffed trash can. "This is the last load." Mike helped her haul the trash to the dumpster behind the school.

"Let's go!" Megan shouted.

Within minutes, they had crossed the Tappan Zee Bridge and were out of the city. Suddenly, the world changed from man-made to God-made. Blue skies, a pale midday sun, and snow-covered evergreens turned the New York State Thruway into a winter wonderland. They sang, laughed, and shared anecdotes about past Christmases. And as Mike recognized landmarks along the way, he kept Megan entertained with an abundance of interesting trivia.

"These mountains are called the Catskills," he said at one point. "Washington Irving immortalized them in his books. Remember old Rip Van Winkle?"

"Wait a minute—back up. You called those foothills mountains?" Megan acted surprised.

"Hey, don't laugh at our mountains." His lower lip protruded into a pout. "Wait till you see the Adirondacks."

"How high are they? Six hundred feet instead of four hundred?"

"Well," he huffed, "at least our mountains aren't bald like yours in New Mexico!"

"Bald?"

"Yeah, bald!"

The miles sped by. Their lighthearted mood deepened as the

subject shifted to plans for the future.

"I've applied to a graduate school in Michigan," Megan said. "And you know, I read they have a great master's program for ministers, too."

Mike frowned. "I really don't know where God wants me right now. I wish I did." Megan looked at him in surprise. What Mike should do seemed perfectly clear to *her*. Surely he would want to complete his seminary training at the same university she'd be attending. This would give their relationship time to grow. *Perhaps God needs a little more time to steer him in that direction,* she reasoned, smiling to herself.

She leaned her head back against the seat and closed her eyes. It was so refreshing to be dating a man who truly believed that success means "waiting on the Lord," not climbing the corporate ladder; a man more concerned about nurturing his connection with God than nurturing the right business contacts. Megan felt good about it. So good, in fact, she fell asleep. And dreamed.

She didn't know how long since she closed her eyes, but when she straightened and stretched, they'd left the New York State Thruway at Albany and were heading north on Interstate 87.

Midwinter twilight had passed when they turned off at the South Glens Falls exit.

"We've about 10 miles left to go now," Mike said. "Remember the novelist James Fenimore Cooper and his book, *The Last of the Mohicans?* Well, the caves where the frontiersmen hid from the Indians are directly under this bridge." He pointed ahead. "My dad and I used to explore them on Sabbath afternoon when I was a kid."

"Really? That's incredible." Megan glanced over at him and shook her head. "I'm impressed. I never knew you were such a history buff."

Mike eyed her thoughtfully. "There's a lot about me you don't know."

She cast him a wry smile. *Thanks Lord, I needed to be reminded of that. We've been together so often these last few months, it's easy to forget that it takes time to build a lasting friendship.*

At last Mike pulled the car to a stop in front of a green, two-story farmhouse.

"Here we are!" He jumped out of the car.

"Here goes." Megan took a deep breath and opened the door. All her self-doubts pushed their way into her mind. *Will his parents like me? What about his grandmother? And his younger sister, Kim? How will she respond to her big brother's new girl friend? How many other girls has he brought home to visit? He's right,* she mused. *There is so much about him I don't know.*

Immediately Megan found herself face-to-face with the largest, slobbering mouth she'd ever seen—except maybe for Amby, her horse. Her surprised look caused Mike to burst out laughing.

"Come here, Sable!" he called. At the sound of the familiar voice, the huge Labrador bounded over into Mike's outstretched arms. They went sprawling into the nearest snowbank. As Megan watched them joyfully wrestle out their greetings, the porch light came on, the screen door banged and a flash of blue jeans hurtled into the fray.

"Mike! Mike, you're home," squealed a young teenage girl, who was obviously glad to see her brother.

The outline of a large man emerged from behind a parked truck, casting a long shadow over the driveway. He walked toward Megan.

"Hi there, I'm Wil, Mike's dad," he smiled. "You must be Megan." The towering man extended a giant work-worn hand and helped her from the car. "Come on in the house. Mama is antsy to meet ya'."

When Megan glanced back over her shoulder at the tussle in the snow, Wil laughed. "Don't pay them no mind. They'll get tired soon enough and join us in the kitchen like civilized folks. Either that or the cold will get to 'em."

He led her up the steps onto the porch where a rounded little woman stood waiting. "This here's Mike's mama, Susan."

"I'm Megan."

"I thought as much," the woman smiled. "Come on, let's get out of the cold."

The warmth of the comfortably cluttered living room made Megan feel right at home. Two mismatched rockers and a leatherette recliner stood against one wall. A brown cotton printed couch with a matching easy chair stood against the other. Framed Americana prints hung on the walls, accenting the wood tones of the two maple end tables by the sofa. At the far end of the room, an old upright piano filled the space between a twinkling Christmas tree and a narrow, lace-paneled window. Formal portraits and casual snapshots of various family members covered the top of the piano.

"Now Wil, get that boy in here with Megan's things while I show her where she'll be staying," Susan ordered as she led Megan to a dimly lit stairwell. "I imagine you're a mite hungry after your drive up from the city. I always hate making that trip! Vegetable stew has been simmering in my Crockpot all day." The woman darted from topic to topic without a break.

"Yum! That sounds good right now," Megan admitted. She followed the older woman up the stairs and down a short hallway.

"I hope you won't mind bunking with Kim for the next few days," Susan went on, turning into one of the bedrooms.

"Oh, no, Mrs. Feldman, that will be just fine, I assure you."

Susan stopped and wagged her finger in Megan's face. "Now we won't have any of that Mrs. Feldman stuff. I'm Susan and my husband's Wil, understand?"

Megan nodded enthusiastically. "Oh yes, Mrs., er, Susan." She smiled to herself. *What a fiesty lady—a bundle of energy, for sure.* Yet in spite of Susan's apparent good humor, Megan sensed a wariness in the woman. *Distrust maybe?* she wondered.

"Kim usually sleeps in the bed on the right," Susan went on. "The bathroom is next door. I'll go on down to the kitchen and set the table while you freshen up."

When Susan disappeared down the stairs, Megan bounced a couple of times on the edge of her bed. The plump red and yellow crazy quilt made it irresistible. A multicolored braid rug linked the two beds with the antique dresser and oval mirror against the wall. An equally ancient padded rocker stood by a matching window seat on the opposite wall. A collection of dolls and stuffed animals on the window seat reminded Megan of her own home so many miles away. She ran her hand over the polished wooden headboard and sighed. How strange to celebrate Christmas among strangers rather than at home with her father.

"Mama says supper's ready and I'm starved." Mike burst into the room with her suitcases. Setting them down by the bed, he bent down and kissed her cheek. "So don't dawdle, ya' hear?"

"Me?" Megan tapped her fingers in fake irritation. "I wasn't the one romping in the snow, remember?"

"Ha! She got you there." Kim was standing near the door giggling. "I think I'm gonna' like this one."

"This one?" Megan walked over to Kim and linked an arm in hers. "Hmmm. So there have been others, huh? How about you and I having a little talk later?" Mike rolled his eyes and chuckled.

In the days that followed, Megan discovered that while the temperatures might be lower and the snow deeper, life on an upstate New York farm wasn't much different from that on a New Mexican range. Mike's parents seemed relaxed and obviously loved each other very much. Wil reminded Megan of her own father, and Kim followed her around like a kid sister. By the second day, Megan felt right at home. Kim even started styling her hair like Megan's. Only in Susan did Megan sense a continued reserve.

On Christmas morning, Megan called her father and Libby to wish them a Merry Christmas. "So how's it going, Meggy darlin'," her father asked. "I sure do miss having you home for the holidays."

"I know, Daddy," she said softly, winding and unwinding the telephone cord about her fingers. "I miss being with you too. You should see all the snow here—like a scene from Currier and Ives."

"We're supposed to get flurries down here too. Won't amount to anything though, I'm sure," he drawled. "So when do I get to meet this fella' of yours?"

"I-I don't exactly know. Soon, perhaps," she stammered self-consciously. Mike and his family in the next room could hear her every word. "Maybe we could talk about it later."

"OK, darlin'," he chuckled. "It's been good hearing from you, kiddo. Libby sends her love."

"Tell her I love her too. Give Amby an extra cube of sugar for me, OK?" She paused. "I love you, Daddy." Megan held the receiver long in her hand after she heard the click at the other end of the line.

Christmas week passed quickly, and before she knew it Mike was packing the car for their return to New York the next morning.

"I don't know if I can bear to go back to the noise of the city," Megan said. "I wish we could stay longer."

"Well, if we don't get a move on you might get your wish," Mike said. "I heard on the news a big snowstorm is coming our way from Canada. It's supposed to dump snow from here to Virginia. But if we get an early start tomorrow morning, I think we can beat it."

"I don't know, son." Wil was worried. "These northeasters can be mighty tricky. Better wait until sunup to decide whether or not to go."

"I don't really have a choice, Dad," Mike said. "Pastor Ulrich is expecting me to cover for him Sabbath."

Mike's dad stroked his chin for a moment. "Well, son, ya' can't buck Mother Nature. Like it or not, she'll have the last say."

Mike decided they should all turn in early that evening, but as Megan readied herself for bed, Kim wanted to talk.

"So just how serious are you and Mike?" she asked. "And don't try to smoke me. I see the way you guys look at each other."

Megan swallowed. "Kim, we started dating only a month ago."

"That doesn't mean anything and you know it," Kim chided.

"Ask your brother." Megan laughed and slipped beneath the covers. "How about we get some sleep now?"

When the alarm went off the next morning, she hopped out of bed, ran to the window, and pulled back the white ruffled curtain. A few gentle flakes were drifting down from the predawn sky. She showered and dressed, then joined Mike and his parents around the breakfast table.

"The snowstorm's expected to hit the Glens Falls area by noon today and continue through tomorrow or Tuesday," Mike told her. "If we don't get out this morning, we may be stuck here until Wednesday or Thursday."

She slipped into the empty chair beside him. "Stuck? Here? Oh, that might not be so bad." Megan glanced up at Susan, smiling. Susan chuckled. Then turning to Mike she said, "It's up to you. You know the weather in these parts better than I. If it were a blizzard coming in off the desert back home, I'd stay put for sure; they can be deadly."

Mike rose from the table and stood looking out the window for a moment. He turned to Megan. "I think we ought to go."

Kim straggled in at the end of their conversation. "So, you gonna' stay until the weekend?"

" 'Fraid not, kiddo." Mike tousled her hair. With the decision made, the family moved to action.

"While you two get ready, I'll fix up a thermos of hot tomato soup," Susan suggested. "Daddy, you'd better put two of our sleeping bags in the back seat in case the car breaks down. At least they won't freeze to death stranded along the highway."

"Got any extra cash, son, in case the car does give you trouble?" his father asked.

"I'm sure I have enough." Mike thumped his father on the back. "Thanks, Dad."

Kim glanced at Megan's sweatshirt and lightweight jacket. Without a word, she ran upstairs to Mike's room and returned with a homemade, bulky-knit wool ski sweater. "Here, this will keep you warm no matter how cold it gets."

Susan made a stack of sandwiches, filled a plastic bag with cookies, selected some fruit and other holiday leftovers and stuffed them into a picnic basket. She handed it to Mike.

"Oh, Ma," he groaned. "The New York State Thruway does have

restaurants along the way, you know."

"No back talk, now," she sputtered. "I just wish you'd wait and go tomorrow or Wednesday."

"I know, I know," Mike conceded. Wil held out his arms and gathered them into a circle.

"Let's ask God to ride with you," he said. As Wil prayed for their safe journey, Megan could feel the family's warmth and love, even for her, a stranger.

Mike and Megan hopped into the car amid a flurry of waves and hugs. Turning out of the driveway they headed for the highway. Mike turned on the radio to a local news station.

A cold light filtered down through layers of ominous storm clouds. Large lazy snowflakes flitted across the windshield playing a gentle game of tag with the wiper blades. By the time Mike and Megan reached the main highway, the lazy flakes had been replaced by a more steady snowfall.

"It's getting worse, huh?" Megan commented. "Should we turn back?"

"The snow's not sticking to the road surface. I still think we can outrun the storm." For a while, they seemed to be doing just that, but a few miles north of Albany, the storm hit with a frenzy. Within minutes, a layer of wet, soggy snow covered the roadway making the asphalt as slick as black ice. The wipers no longer cleared the windshield. Mike slowed the car. Creeping along with visibility cut to only a few dozen feet, Mike gingerly steered around other, less cautious drivers, who had slipped off the roadway into deep snow.

"Poor people," Megan said. "I wish we could do something for them."

"The best thing we can do now is keep moving," Mike said. "If we stop we'll be stuck, too. Look!" He pointed ahead. "A trucker jackknifed in the median."

A large tractor-trailer rig had spilled into the deep snow along the roadside and now sat immobilized. Traffic had already begun to snarl around it as people tried to inch their way past.

"Those guys really have it tough in snow like this," Mike said. "As long as they can keep going straight, they're OK. All that weight gives them great traction. But try to stop or turn too fast and it's all over."

"I don't like this, Mike," Megan told him shakily. "Maybe we should go back."

"We've come too far to turn around now," Mike explained. "Besides, the main part of the storm is behind us. Going back will be worse than this." He squinted at the glaring white wall of snow swirling around them. "If we take it slow, I think we'll be OK. Anyway, we haven't got a choice."

Megan shivered. "This sure reminds me of the blizzards we sometimes get in New Mexico. Once a neighbor froze to death just ten feet from his own back door."

They inched forward in a long line of passenger cars, barely able to make out the taillights of the vehicle in front of them or the headlights of the car behind. One by one, the cars pulled off the highway. But Mike pressed on.

"Maybe we should pull off, too," Megan offered. "This is really scaring me."

"I would, but then what?" Mike shrugged. "We'll be buried for sure. It might take a couple of days to get out. Are you prepared for that?" He looked at her with a sly grin. Megan ignored him.

She stared into the blinding snow, then glanced at Mike. *Once he gets an idea into his head, he doesn't let go,* she thought. *Just like Dad.* She smiled. How many times during her growing up years she'd said the same thing about him. She wondered how she could both admire and yet be frustrated by the very same trait.

Suddenly, across the median, there was trouble. An impatient driver whipped his car around a lumbering tractor-trailer that blocked his way. Hardly had he cleared the bumper of the towering rig than he turned sharply in front of it. On a dry surface such a maneuver would have been, at best, inconsiderate. But on the slick, snow-covered roadway, it spelled certain disaster.

The trucker jammed on his brakes to avoid plowing into the car. Immediately the rig began to spin out of control. The trailer slid crazily across the lanes of traffic. A second car, coming up from behind, swerved into the median to avoid colliding with the trailer. Hopelessly out of control, the driver skidded across the median straight toward Mike's car.

"Look out!" Megan shouted. Headlights from the other car glared into the windshield. Mike turned sharply to avoid the impact, but too late. "Oh, dear Jesus!" Megan whispered.

She heard the sound of brakes digging into loose gravel, metal ripping through metal, and glass shattering around her—then blessed quietness.

CHAPTER

8

Flashes of red and blue light pulsated to the throb of the pain in Megan's head. She attempted to open her eyes, but could not. The stench of gasoline fumes filled the air. She felt terribly cold, and her teeth were chattering uncontrollably. Somewhere far in the distance she could hear wailing sirens and shouting voices. *Where am I?* she wondered. *What has happened to me?* She struggled to sit up, but strong hands held her back. She tried to speak, but no words came. She could dimly feel a plastic mask covering her nose and mouth.

"I—I can't breathe!" Far away she heard someone groan in pain. She tried to reach out to help, but couldn't move.

"Sh-sh-sh," a distant voice comforted. "Just lie still. She's coming to." Suddenly everything faded away. The voices, the lights, the sirens, and the pain—all disappeared under a soothing blanket of darkness. Megan felt as if she were floating in a world of downy comfort.

She sensed rather than saw that she was in an ambulance. *Why?* she wondered. *I feel fine.* Yet she knew she wasn't fine. She hurt, but she wasn't sure quite where or why. Then out of the misty darkness of her mind came the glare of headlights, the sound of rending metal, the snow, the car. *Oh, Mike!* her mind screamed. *Mike, where are you?* She shuddered and the warm blanket of oblivion returned.

Megan surfaced again. She tried to open her eyes but her eyelids felt as heavy as lead. Somewhere she could hear a man and a woman talking. She turned her head and tried to focus on who was speaking. It was like watching a soap opera on television. *Paramedics. But of course.* She smiled to herself. *They must be taking her to a hospital.*

Suddenly she began shivering. *Oh, it's cold—so cold.* Her teeth chattered.

"She's going into shock, Jeff," the female attendant called. "I can't stabilize her. Can you go any faster?"

"I'm going as fast as I can," a voice from behind Megan's head replied. "The road's too icy. Besides, I can't see more than 10 feet in front of me. The snow's already covered up the tracks from Hank's ambulance and he pulled out less than three minutes before us."

"Sure hope the other one makes it," the first voice replied. "He was pretty banged up."

The other one? Megan's mind cleared momentarily. *She must mean Mike! Mike is hurt!* She tried to speak, but made only weak groans. Frustrated, she tried again. *Listen to me! Is Mike all right?* Again, only a faint whimper.

"Sh-sh-sh, relax." The woman stroked her arm. "You're gonna' be just fine."

It's Mike I'm worried about, not me! Megan struggled to speak but her mouth wouldn't form the right syllables. She tried to concentrate but her head hurt too much to think. The insulating blanket of darkness once again covered her, quelling her troubling thoughts.

When Megan awoke, it was still dark. She didn't know how long she'd slept. Perhaps she'd just dozed off for a few minutes. Or perhaps she'd spent hours, days, or weeks lost in the haze of pain. She neither knew nor cared. She was in a bed. A sheet and mattress pad beneath her rustled as she tried to move. But something held her down. Her conscious mind dimly tried to analyze what it might be. She opened her eyes and tried to focus on her surroundings. *Where am I? At the ranch? At Mama Grace's? At Mike's place?*

Megan could hear muffled sounds of people talking, moving, carts rolling about outside the darkened room. A bright light shone under the door. Then she knew. In her mind she could see Mike, his parents, snow pelting a car windshield. Suddenly glaring headlights were heading straight for her! *Mike look out!*

Megan lay rigid for several minutes gasping, sweating. Slowly, she calmed down again. *Mike,* she thought. *What happened to Mike?* A kind of fog was slowly lifting from her mind. Her thoughts began to connect, to make sense. *I must be on some kind of pain medication to be so groggy,* she thought. *If I'm in a hospital bed, there must be a pager here. I can call a nurse or somebody.* She thrashed her hand about trying to locate the call button. Suddenly the night-light above her bed switched on. Megan blinked. *Got it!*

Moments later, a young woman about Megan's own age smiled down at her. "Hello there, Miss Daniels. Is anything wrong? May I get you something?"

Megan licked her parched lips. "I'm very thirsty. May I have a drink of water?"

"Of course." The woman held up a glass allowing Megan to sip the icy cold water through a plastic straw. "My name is Cathy and I'm your nurse for the night shift. May I do anything else for you?"

"Can you tell me where I am?"

"Sure. You're at the Capitol Medical Center in Albany, New York. You were in a car accident on the New York Thruway yesterday afternoon," the nurse explained. "Do you remember anything about it?"

"Vaguely." Megan reached up with her right hand and touched the bandage covering her forehead. A sharp pain ripped through the lower right side of her chest. She winced. "At least I think so."

"Good. Dr. Haas will be glad to hear it. Now you lay quiet while I tell him you are awake." The nurse bustled out of the room. Seconds later she returned with a sandy-haired young man wearing a white medical coat over blue jeans. He looked very tired, yet the doctor's eyes sparkled with friendliness.

"So, Miss Daniels, you finally decided to wake up, huh? I'm Dr. Haas at your service. Let's see how you're doing." He checked her pulse and listened to her heart sounds. When he finished, Dr. Haas pulled the covers up and patted her arm. "You got a pretty nasty bump on your head there, Miss Daniels. But as concussions go, yours is relatively mild. You've got three broken ribs on the right side here, but they look fine right now. You'll be back in your jazzercise class in no time. The good news is your vital signs are stabilized. You really gave us a scare a couple of times yesterday."

"When can I leave?"

"Leave? You just got here." He laughed. "Don't worry. In a couple of days or so, if everything keeps mending nicely, you'll be on your way."

"What about Mike, the driver of the car I was in? Is he all right?"

The doctor shrugged. "I'm sorry, I really don't know. But I'll try to find out for you later this morning, OK?"

Megan nodded her head slowly. "What time is it?"

The doctor glanced at his watch. "It's 5:45 in the morning."

"Four, three—" Megan figured the time difference between

New York and Albuquerque. "Would it be all right for me to call my father?"

"Sure." Dr. Haas stood up. "Nurse Collins can help you. However, don't talk too long, you hear? You need your rest." He grinned, patted her arm, and left the room.

I won't cry! I won't cry, Megan told herself. The nurse placed the call for Megan, then handed her the receiver. Megan listened as the phone rang once, twice, three times. After the fifth ring, she heard the answering machine click on. Her father's familiar voice came onto the line. "You have reached the Daniels' residence . . ." Tears slipped from Megan's eyes as the recorded message continued.

She gulped back her tears and cleared her throat. "Daddy," she told the machine, "there's been an accident. I'm OK, but I need to talk to you." She left the name and number of the hospital and hung up the receiver.

The nurse helped her get comfortable. "Now, how about you get some serious rest before the morning shift comes on duty."

Megan reached up and gripped Cathy's forearm. "Are you sure you can't tell me anything about Mike?"

The woman shook her head sadly. "I've been with you all night so I really don't know. But one thing is certain. Worrying won't change anything. The best thing you can do right now is get some rest."

Megan fell back against the pillow and closed her eyes. It hurt to think. When she opened them, she was alone again. An abstract design of morning light streaming through the window splashed across the foot of her bed.

"Hi," a woman's voice called to her from the doorway. "How are you feeling?"

Megan peered into the shadows. "Susan?" The woman moved to the side of the bed. Megan was right. It was Susan. Tired, worn, but no matter. A familiar face at last.

"How are you feeling?" Susan asked.

"Me? I—uh—I'm fine, I think. When did you get here?"

Susan adjusted the sheet and blanket about Megan's shoulders. "Wil and I drove down as soon as we received the call about the accident."

"The accident . . . oh, yes, the accident," Megan remembered. "How's Mike? What happened to Mike? No one will tell me."

The woman squeezed Megan's hand. "He's been in surgery most of the night. They have him in Intensive Care right now. The surgeon assured us everything went as well as could be expected."

"As well as could be expected?" Megan struggled to sit up. "What's that supposed to mean?"

"We're just not sure yet." Susan wrung her hands helplessly. "The other car hit Mike's door almost head on, so Mike took the brunt of the impact. He broke some bones in the left arm and shoulder but . . ." The woman swallowed hard. "His back, that's what took so long in surgery. His spine has been injured, but they don't know how badly yet. You just can't tell with these things, I guess."

"Oh, no . . ." Megan gasped. Her mind struggled to understand Susan's words.

Susan blinked back her tears. "Anyway, Wil suggested I come up to see you while we wait for Mike to regain consciousness. They told us you were still asleep, but I came on in anyway."

Megan stared up at the ceiling. "When will they know if, if the surgery was successful?"

"They're not making any promises." Susan dabbed at her eyes with a facial tissue.

"What happened to the driver of the other car?" Megan asked.

"He was only 16 years old; just got his license a few weeks ago. He wasn't wearing a seat belt, and . . ." Susan looked away. "I am so grateful Mike is alive, I really am." Hastily she strode to the window and looked out. "Oh, dear God," she breathed, "I am grateful." Then she began to cry. Sobbing, she slumped into an armchair and buried her face in her hands.

Megan tried to reach for the grieving woman, but her movement sent a shot of pain through her side. She slumped back against the pillow. "Oh, Susan, I-I-I . . ." Megan wanted to say something to comfort her, something to give her hope, but no words came.

The door opened and a nurse appeared. "Ready for a little breakfast?" she asked, carrying in a small tray of food. Then she saw Susan slumped in the chair. "Oh, I'm sorry. I'll come back later."

Susan stood up and took a deep breath. "Never mind. I need to get back to my son. I want to be there when he awakens." She reached over and patted Megan's arm. "Wil will drop by later today to see how you're doing." Then she left.

The hospital's morning routine kept Megan from dwelling on the tragedy. She allowed herself to be bathed, fed, prodded, and administered to by hospital personnel. She had just settled back against her freshly plumped pillows when the door swung open again and a giant stuffed panda bear popped his head around the door jamb, followed by her father's face. Megan's jaw dropped open.

"Hi there, Meggy darlin'." Herb sauntered to the side of the bed and plopped the stuffed animal on her stomach. "So, what'cha doin' lazin' around in bed at this hour of the day? Time's a wastin', you know. Why the day's half gone."

Megan stared in shock. "But-but-but-but!"

He laughed and planted a kiss on her cheek. "Why, child, you sound like our old tractor trying to kick over on a cold winter morning. Not surprising seeing how cold it is in these parts."

"But-but-but—"

"There you go again. So what kind of welcome is this? Aren't you going to give me a kiss and a hug?" She reached for him, but winced at the pain in her side. His eyes saddened for a moment as he bent toward her. "At least a kiss, anyway."

She kissed his rough cheek, still uncertain if this was all real or just the medication giving her wild dreams. But no, the rough callouses on his palms, the fine layer of blond hairs on the back of his hand, the scent of the outdoors; this was no dream. "Daddy . . ." she wailed. Tears slid down her face. She pulled him closer. "You're here! In New York."

"Of all places!" His tears mixed with hers as he kissed her fingertips one at a time. "Tell me, where else would I be when my little girl needs me? I caught the first plane east as soon as I heard from the Feldmans."

"And Libby? Is she here too?"

"No, somebody had to take care of the ranch. But she insists I bring you home to recuperate. When does the doctor say you'll be ready to leave the hospital?"

"A day or two, I guess." Home—Megan couldn't think of any place she'd rather be than to be surrounded by the safe, familiar world of New Mexico.

She listened as her father told her about his flight east and laughed as he described maneuvering his rental car through Albany's narrow, snow-covered streets. As she listened, she wondered about her students back in New York. *Had they heard about the accident too? Who was going to teach them now?*

Later that day when the nurse arrived to administer medications, she cautioned Megan to get some rest. Megan's father suggested he look up the Feldmans and see how Mike was doing. "I need to check into a motel close by and give Libby a call too. But I'll be back to see you tonight during regular visiting hours. You get some sleep, you hear?" He kissed her again and left.

"Would it be possible for me to see my friend, Mike Feldman?" Megan asked the nurse.

"Probably not today." The woman handed Megan a glass of water and two capsules. "But I'll see what I can arrange for tomorrow, all right?"

That night her father arrived as soon as visiting hours began. At the end of the evening, the Feldmans stopped by to report on Mike's condition.

"He's conscious, but groggy from the pain medication," Wil explained. "But it's still too soon to know if there's any paralysis. The specialist says that Mike was lucky. None of the nerves in his lower back were actually severed, just crushed together. He said these nerve roots can stand a lot more trauma than those of the upper spinal cord and often regenerate."

Megan's father nodded solemnly. "At least there's hope." The two men continued talking with one another as Megan glanced over at Susan who was staring out of the window. Megan tried to draw her into the conversation, but it was as if the woman didn't hear. She stood silent, lost in her own thoughts. After a few minutes, they left.

"Mike will be OK, Daddy. I just know it." Megan nodded her head emphatically. "I've prayed about it and I have faith that he'll be just fine."

Her father massaged Megan's free hand gently. "I hope you're right, sweetheart."

Disbelief and anger rose within her. She jerked her hand free. "Don't you believe?"

Megan's father smiled down at his daughter. "I believe in the power of prayer, but our prayers must always include a 'Thy will be done.'" He paused and stroked Megan's cheek for a moment. "Only God knows what is best for Michael—for any of us for that matter. To that end, we must pray."

"I know, Daddy, but certainly God wants Michael to walk again. After all, he's training to become a minister. He wouldn't leave Mike—" Tears blinded her once again. She couldn't finish her thought.

"You're right. God promised He would never leave nor forsake Mike. Regardless of the outcome, He will keep that promise."

Megan shook her head back and forth. "You're leaving room for doubt. No, Daddy, I won't even consider the possibility that God won't heal him completely." She clenched her fists and frowned. "To even harbor such a thought would demonstrate a lack of faith. James 1:6 warns us to ask in faith, nothing wavering. Nothing wavering!"

He nodded slowly. His face lined with concern for his daughter. "I remember saying the same thing when your mama first learned she had cancer." He bent down and kissed Megan on her bandaged forehead. "We'll talk some more tomorrow, Meggy darlin'—tomorrow."

CHAPTER

9

The frozen world beyond Megan's hospital window sparkled in the late morning sunlight. Every tree in the park below wore a radiant robe of crystal. The sidewalks glistened. Megan shivered and turned away from the window. For the first time in her life, the beauty of winter left her feeling bitter and hostile.

She crossed the hospital room and peered into the mirror above the vanity sink. The doctor had replaced the heavy bandage on her forehead with a smaller one. Angry bruises darkened the right side of her face where she'd hit the doorframe of Mike's car. Her hair fell limp and straggly around her shoulders, showing little evidence of the shampoo and rinse she had subjected herself to that morning. She winced at the pain in her side as she smoothed a stray lock of hair in place. She picked up her compact and applied a fresh layer of powder in an attempt to cover up her blackened eye. It didn't help.

"Ready to go?" The door opened and an orderly named Lonnie pushed an empty wheelchair into the room. "Your limo is waiting." With a flourish he gestured at the seat..

"Really, I can walk down to third floor just fine," she protested.

"Sorry, hospital rules. We can't have our guests slipping on our tile floors, can we?"

"I guess I don't have a choice, huh?" she asked.

The attendant grinned. "You got it." Megan slipped into the chair. She felt silly. Lonnie chattered on. "You'd be surprised how many patients feel just like you. Why me? After pushing as many of these contraptions around as I do all day, I'd sit back and enjoy it." He skillfully manuevered her down the hall to the elevator.

When they reached third floor, Megan asked the orderly to stop for a moment outside Mike's room. "Is my hair all right? I mean, as all right as it can be under the circumstances?" She flipped it back off her shoulders, then straightened her red flannel robe.

Lonnie grinned. "I think you look exquisite. I wish you were dropping by to see me."

She grinned and shook her head. "I look like a train wreck. But thanks anyway."

The young man pushed the door open and bowed graciously. "We aim to please, Ma'am."

Through the doorway, Megan caught her first glimpse of Mike's inert form stretched out on a bed. She gasped. Machines that beeped and blinked surrounded the headboard. Tubes came out of his arms to the machines and to half-empty bottles hanging from poles attached to his bed. A brace held his head and body stationary. Oxygen tanks stood silently to one side. Even the look in his drug-induced gaze seemed strange and unfamiliar. Flowers and mylar balloons surrounded his bed. The windowsill and his bedside table were cluttered with colorful "get well" cards. *Someone knows we're here,* she thought.

"Help me out of this thing," Megan whispered to the attendant. Susan sat on the opposite side of the bed brushing Mike's hair from his forehead while his father, Wil, stood at the end of the bed.

"Well, hello, stranger!" Wil smiled broadly. "So they finally let you out, eh?" Megan nodded.

"Still have to be carted around, though," she gestured at Lonnie. "I've got my own private chauffeur." Lonnie bowed in greeting, then headed for the door. "I'll be back later to take you back. Just give me a call." Megan moved to the foot of Mike's bed.

"Hi, Mike." She tried to sound casual. Mike glanced at her for a moment.

"Hi," he said at last. Wil coughed lightly and turned to his wife.

"Susan, why don't you and I take a walk down to the cafeteria? I hear they have a great salad bar."

"I-I-I'd rather not." The woman edged closer to her son. "Michael may need something."

"Megan can get it." Wil took Susan by the arm. "Come on now, you haven't eaten in hours. You've got to keep your strength up." The woman glared at her husband. Her lips tightened into a defiant line. For a moment they stared fixedly at each other. Then Susan sighed, turned quickly, and strode from the room. Wil followed. As the door closed behind them, Megan inched closer to the bed.

"So how are you doing?" She reached out and took his hand.

He glanced first at her then at the ceiling. "The doctors say I'm doing as well as can be expected."

"I didn't ask what the doctors say. I want to know how you feel."

He closed his eyes. "I'm not sure yet. So much has happened. How about you?"

"I'm OK. My doctor says I'll be released tomorrow."

"Are you going back to New Mexico with your father?"

Megan thought for a moment. "I don't know." She smiled. "I have a teaching contract until the end of the school year, remember?"

He frowned and drew his lips together. "You really should go, you know."

"Huh! You're going to need someone around to hound you and keep you humble, what with all the pretty nurses in this hospital fawning all over you," she teased.

Mike closed his eyes for a moment. "Yeah, right! Look, Megan, I'm a little tired. Could you come back later, perhaps?"

"Of course, I understand." She kissed him gently and patted his shoulder. "You just get well, ya' hear?" His eyes remained closed as she slipped out the door where Lonnie and her wheelchair were waiting.

"That was quick," he said good-naturedly.

"He's pretty tired." Megan tried to sound hopeful. "I think he needs to rest a while." As they headed back to her room, Megan's mind tried to absorb all she had seen. *Mike is pretty banged up, no question,* she thought. *Both inside and out.*

She had just sat down on the edge of the bed when her father arrived. "Hey, I heard the good news. They're letting you out of here tomorrow." He studied her face for a moment. "You don't look too happy over the prospect."

Megan's eyes misted. She took a tissue from the box beside her bed and dabbed her eyes. "I just got back from visiting Mike. He looks awful."

"I know." Her father glanced down at the floor.

She paced to the window and stared out at a snowplow passing on the street below. "And he's not himself at all. Something's going on inside him that he's not telling."

"Megan, sit down." Her father guided her to the visitor's chair. "Mike has good reasons for not acting like himself. Right now, I imagine he's not sure just who or what he is. He's put a lot of confidence in the physical therapy ahead, and sometimes miracles do happen. I'm sure

Mike is hoping for such a miracle, but there are no guarantees."

"No! That's not fair!" Megan shook her head. "God wouldn't allow something like that to happen." Mike permanently paralyzed? What would this do to their love for one another, a love too young to survive the cold, harsh, reality of such a disaster? They needed time to build a strong relationship, time to laugh, time to play, time to— She threw herself into her father's outstretched arms and cried.

He ran his hand over her hair and whispered, "Megan, honey, who ever said life was fair?"

"God will heal him. He will!" Megan shouted, startling both her father and herself with her vehement reaction.

"I hope so, baby. I really hope so."

Guilt flooded through her as she stared at her father's ashen face and recognized an old, familiar pain in his eyes.

"Oh, Daddy . . ." Megan's body shook with uncontrollable sobs. "Please, God. Please do something!"

"Meggy darlin'." He took her in his arms. She clung to him with a fierceness she'd never felt before. "Don't tie God's hands. He knows what He's doing."

The next day she was to go home. Before leaving the hospital with her father, she arranged to visit Mike once more. He seemed to be feeling a little better this morning—almost his old self. More hand drawn get-well cards, letters, and flowers decorated his room. The members of his church, from the youngest to the oldest, had sent their greetings.

"So, you are going back to New Mexico with your dad?" He sounded disinterested, as if he really didn't care one way or the other.

Megan eyed him strangely. "Hey, are you trying to get rid of me or something? You asked me the same question yesterday."

"Oh, yeah," he sighed and looked past her at the ceiling. "Well, give everyone my love and thank them for their prayers."

She smiled down at the solemn eyes that had always sparkled with so much happiness. "Anything you want me to bring you from the city when I come back to see you next weekend? Bagels? New York Cheesecake? Mama Grace's chili?"

He closed his eyes. "Megan, don't come back. Get on with your life. It's going to be months, maybe years before I'm a whole man again."

"I beg your pardon?" She stared at him in shock. "Are you serious?" Quietly, Megan's father excused himself from the room.

"I have never been more serious in my life." Mike's eyes hardened;

his lips tightened in a thin line. "You are a beautiful and vibrant woman, and I am only half a man. You deserve more than I can possibly give you at this time, possibly at any time."

"Whoa there. What are you talking about?" Megan's hands flew up in protest. "We are friends, you and I—best of friends. We have a friendship that will last a lifetime. Don't sell me or our friendship short."

"Don't you understand what I'm trying to tell you?" Tears of frustration sprang into Mike's eyes. "I've spent the last few days being poked, prodded, tested, and retested by an unending succession of doctors, surgeons, and physical therapists. From what they tell me, I'll never be the same again."

Megan's eyes flashed steely gray. In a low, controlled voice she said, "I know perfectly well what you are saying and what you are not saying, Michael. I took anatomy and physiology in college, remember? I understand how the male body works!" His face reddened but he remained silent. "Which is neither here nor there as far as we are concerned." She clenched her fists. "So don't go playing martyr with me, Michael Feldman. I refuse to allow you to throw us away. Now, if you have nothing more constructive to say to me, my dad is waiting to drive me back to Mama Grace's." She leaned over and placed a firm "don't mess with me" kiss on his lips and walked from the room.

The door closed behind her. Megan wrapped her arms about herself, trying to stop shaking. Her father drew her into his arms.

"It's all right, honey. Go ahead and cry." Tears tumbled down her face onto his suede jacket.

"I thought I cried myself dry last night," she said, her voice breaking on every syllable.

"I know. I know," her father soothed as he handed her a clean handkerchief. Lonnie helped her settle into the waiting wheelchair while her father carried her things. When they reached the lobby, her father went for his rental car while Lonnie wheeled her out into the bright sunlight. She took a greedy breath of fresh air. Everything looked so glorious after the days spent closed away in a cheerless hospital room.

Herb pulled the car under the entrance portico. As it turned toward her, she drew back sharply. The memory of crunching metal, shattering glass, and screaming brakes made her feel faint. Her heart raced; her mouth went dry. *Get a grip,* she warned herself. *When you fall off a horse, the best thing to do is to get back on, remember?*

Herb got out of the car and loaded her belongings into the back seat. When he reached over to help her out of the chair, she'd was almost back to normal.

She slid her legs into the front seat and fastened her seat belt. Lonnie waved a final goodbye and closed the car door. *Poor Mike,* she thought to herself. *For him, even the simplest motion such as getting into a car has now become a monumental task.* She turned to Herb as they drove away. "I wish I could have said goodbye to the Feldmans before I left."

"They're meeting with one of Mike's specialists right now," her father said. "I saw them a while ago and told them you were leaving. They send their love."

Megan frowned. "I don't understand Mike's mother. She acts like she resents me."

Her father patted her arm gently. "Don't be too hard on her. She's just a good mama bear protecting her injured cub."

"What does she think I'm going to do—rip the IVs from his arm?"

He threw back his head and laughed. "No, but she just might be afraid that you'll go for his heart."

Megan shook her head, then glanced out of her window. The sun sparkled on a crisp and snowy-white landscape. Driving south, they passed many of the landmarks she had seen on her trip north. She tried to tell her father some of the anecdotes Mike had shared with her, but the lump in her throat kept getting in the way.

"I never realized how pretty the state of New York really is," Herb said. "I guess I thought it was one major urban sprawl." He reached to tune in to an easy listening station on the car radio. "So you think you need to stay in New York instead of coming back to New Mexico with me?" he asked.

"Oh, Daddy, you know I do," Megan said. They had talked about this several times, yet Herb kept asking her about it. "If I don't, who will take over the teaching job at the school? Pastor Ulrich has tried everywhere, but no new teacher can be found. Besides, I made a promise. I can't let them down."

"It's OK, honey." Herb patted her arm. "Can't blame me for trying, though. Why don't you just lean back and close your eyes for a few minutes."

She nodded, swallowing hard. However, when she closed her eyes, all she could see was Mike—laughing, exuberant, on-the-go Mike— lying in a hospital bed attached to tubes, needles, and machines.

The image refused to fade during the days that followed. Megan's father stayed in town for the rest of the week. Though he never mentioned it, she knew he still hoped she'd return with him to New Mexico. His last day there, he took her on a shopping spree. He insisted on buying her three pairs of shoes, two sweaters, jeans, and a jacket to replace the one ruined in the accident. She drew the line when he picked out an expensive red silk Sabbath dress for her.

"My blue suit still fits fine," she urged. "I don't need a new—"

"We're not talking need here," Herb insisted. "Take it from a man who knows, every woman should own a red dress." Finally Megan relented and let him buy the dress. It was lovely.

At last Megan and her father stood at the airline boarding gate. She felt physically ill at the thought of saying goodbye. Herb took her by the arms and looked straight into her eyes.

"Did I ever tell you, Meggy darlin', how proud of you I am for your determination to stick it out here after all that's happened—not that I would ever have expected less from you. You are your mama's girl, you know."

With a final wave, he disappeared down the tunnel into the plane. Megan felt as if she were letting go of the only portion of her life that was secure. She wanted to run after him, go home, back to the familiarity of her childhood, to the open spaces where smoke and concrete didn't blot out the sun and neon lights didn't outshine the stars. Leaving would be so easy—so very easy.

Within the week; she returned to her classroom. Her class had painted a giant mural and taped it to the wall. "Welcome back, Miss Megan!" it said. She noticed that her students used any excuse to sidle up to her, to touch her arm, to tell her how much they missed her.

"My mama told me you weren't coming back," Dina confided, "but I knew better. Pastor Mike will come back too, right?"

Megan brushed a stray curl from the little girl's forehead. "I don't know, Dina. He's still not feeling too well."

"Don't worry, Miss Megan," the first grader whispered into Megan's ear, "I'm praying for him."

Megan's eyes misted as she placed a kiss on the girl's cheek. "I am too."

During the next few weeks, Megan sent daily notes to Mike along with letters and cartoons from the children. He never replied. His mother faithfully answered each of the letters, including Megan's. With each one, she hoped for encouraging news regarding the paralysis.

Instead, Susan always described him as "doing as well as can be expected." While she wanted to visit him, he had told her to stay away. Megan felt she should honor his request.

Life with Mama Grace and the children continued as before. The house constantly buzzed with activity, and Megan usually worked grading papers and making lesson plans until late at night. Yet long after Sara fell asleep each evening, Megan would lay awake for hours thinking about Mike. She missed him more than she cared to admit. Even crazy Sara couldn't make her laugh like he could.

One Thursday evening after supper Mama Grace said, "My sister, Evelyn, lives in South Troy, you know."

"I didn't know that." Megan glanced at Mama Grace. "Is that far from here?"

"South Troy is right across the river from Albany," said Mama Grace. Megan froze. Mama Grace went on. "She sure likes company now that her youngest daughter is back at college." She looked at Megan.

"Oh, that's nice." Feigning innocence Megan asked, "Are you going to visit her soon?"

"No, but you are," Mama Grace shot back. "The way you've been moping about these last few weeks—it's the only cure I know."

"But—" Megan sputtered.

"Take a bus to Albany and rent a car. Shouldn't put you back too much."

"But—" Megan frowned.

"Well?" The woman stood with her hands on her hips. "Should I call Evelyn or not?"

Suddenly Megan's eyes lit up. A smile wreathed her face. "Yes—Yes!" She kissed Mama Grace on the cheek and bounded up the stairs to her room. She flung the door open and announced, "Guess what? I'm going to see Mike this weekend."

"I know." Sara glanced up from the letter she was writing. "I already got your travel case down from the shelf. Take the red dress." Megan stood in the doorway, bewildered.

"How . . . ? " she began.

Sara laughed. "Mama Grace has been planning this for weeks now. I'm supposed to pick you up after school and drive you to the bus station. Mrs. Feldman already knows you're coming."

At the mention of Susan Feldman, Megan froze. Her eyes widened in fear. "What if Mike doesn't want to see me?" she whispered.

"Nonsense!" Sara returned her attention to the letter she'd been writing. "Don't create problems where they don't exist."

Yet they did exist. In all the time since the accident Mike had made no effort to contact her. It could very well be that Mike would refuse to see her after all. The thought nagged at Megan throughout the night and all the next morning. Before Megan could change her mind though, Sara swept her off to the Port Authority bus station and she was on her way to Albany.

Megan watched the trees speed by her window. Only a month ago she'd ridden over this same highway with Mike, yet so much had changed. Even the scenery looked different. Warmer temperatures had melted most of the snow leaving only patches of white throughout the woods. Everything looked dreary and cold. *Just the way I feel,* she thought.

Evelyn proved to be an older version of Mama Grace—a Mama Grace with dimples. The woman seemed to crackle with energy as she whipped about the guest room plumping pillows and straightening the bedspread. But she had little time to visit. Within minutes of arriving at the townhouse, Megan changed into her new red dress as Sara had ordered and headed for the hospital. On her way, she spied a gift shop in a small shopping plaza. She stopped in and purchased ten helium-filled balloons.

As Megan walked down the hospital corridor, painful memories flooded over her. The noxious odor of antiseptics, the charge of tension in the air, the gleaming floors and high gloss walls. With each step her lips tightened and her eyes clouded. She felt sick. She gripped her stomach in an effort to calm her mounting fear. Outside his hospital room door, she paused to whisper a quick prayer. Suddenly, the door flew open and Megan found herself face-to-face with a startled Susan.

The older woman gasped and lifted her finger to her lips. "Sh, Mike doesn't know you're coming." She closed the door behind her. "We need to talk before you see him."

CHAPTER

10

"I-I-I hope I'm not intruding being here, Mrs. Feldman," Megan began. "Mama Grace assured me that you—" Susan motioned for her to keep quiet. Megan obeyed. They walked to the solarium at the end of the hall. In a quiet corner beside a giant, potted palm plant, they sat down.

"If there's a problem . . ." Megan began.

"I'm Susan, remember?" the woman interrupted her. "There's not a problem. In fact, I'm very glad you are here." The woman took a deep breath, then continued. "But I want to apologize for my less than friendly manner last time we met. I guess I was afraid for my son. And if I were totally honest with myself, I'd admit I resented seeing you walk out of here with only minor injuries while its very likely Michael James will never walk again."

"Oh, Susan," Megan stared at the woman. "I understand, I really do. When I first woke up after the accident, I felt guilty too. And I wouldn't hurt Mike. He's my friend."

"I know that now," Susan nodded. "Though he refuses to talk about you, I can tell he misses you terribly. There's a pretty young woman who visits her husband in the room across the hall from his most every day. Her hair color is about the same as yours." Susan stared down at her own hands folded in her lap. "The first few times Mike saw her, he called your name. Now whenever she appears, he turns his face toward the wall. Mothers notice stuff like that, you know."

Megan bit her lip and glanced away. She knew just how Mike was feeling. Many times during the past few weeks her heart had raced at the sight of some stranger walking down the street just the way Mike used to. Or she'd see someone standing at the far end of a subway car, slouching against a pole just like he did. Only it never was Mike. Each time the disappointment she felt cut deeper into her heart.

"So you see," Susan continued, "I'm glad you are here. But there's more—the paralysis. While some feeling has returned to his body, the doctors hold out little hope for him to walk again." She ran her fingers along a seam in her skirt.

"No!" Megan closed her eyes and shook her head back and forth slowly. "No, no, no . . ."

"He's been going to physical therapy and for counseling faithfully, but I can see that he's not really dealing with his problem." Susan went on. "But how can he when just day-to-day living is a battle for survival? He can hardly dress himself, let alone think of the future." Susan held her breath for a moment. "Then there are the pressure sores from too much sitting, too little exercise. He's fighting bladder infections that won't go away. I just don't know where any of us are going from here." She closed her eyes and held two fingers to her lips, as if to quiet her own nagging fears. A few minutes passed before she spoke again. "I may be breaking a trust telling you this." She paused. "When the local pastor or elder comes to visit, or the medical personnel come into the room, Mike adopts a role."

"A role?" Megan blinked back her tears. "I don't understand."

"He becomes the 'good Christian,' saying all the right things, doing all the right things. Everyone marvels at how well he's adjusting to his misfortune. But I know better. As soon as they leave, he reverts into a moody silence—I can't reach him." Susan stood up and stared out the window, her eyes brimming with tears; her knuckles clenched. "I can't reach him. His own mother, and I can't reach him!" Megan searched for something to say but words seemed so trite, so empty. All she could do was listen.

"I haven't known who to talk to. When I talk with Wil, he just says, 'Give the boy time.' Once I tried to confide in the pastor, but he kept going on about what a fine young man I'd raised and how close to God Mike seemed to be." Susan stood silent for several moments.

"You know I'll do everything I can for Mike," Megan said.

Susan wiped away her tears. "I know you will. I can see you really care for him."

"As a friend," Megan warned as she rose to her feet.

Susan smiled and nodded. "Understood—as a friend."

The two women walked back to Mike's room. Susan opened the

door and peeked around the edge. "There's someone here to see you, Mike."

Megan patted out the imaginary wrinkles in the skirt of her dress and breezed into the room. "Hi, Mike." She strolled over to the edge of his bed and thrust the bouquet of balloons into his hand.

"What in the—" He stopped. His jaw dropped open. "Oh! You look fab—" When he reached for her, the balloons floated upward. Megan grabbed for the ribbons, but missed. "What are you doing here? I thought I told you to go back to New Mexico with your dad."

"You did, huh?" Megan's eyes snapped with emotion. She placed her hands defiantly on her hips. "Since when do I take my travel instructions from you?"

"Er, I mean, I suggested—"

"Michael Feldman, don't you ever—I mean ever—presume you can order me about. Is that clear? I'm not your pet turtle!"

"OK, OK. I'm sorry," he mumbled. "I wasn't trying to order you about. I just . . ."

"Besides, if I were in New Mexico, how could I deliver this?" Megan opened her purse and hauled out a roll of cashier's tape, letting it unravel to the floor and under the bed. Names and signatures covered the narrow strip of paper. "Half of New York City send their greetings." She started reading from the top. "Sara and each of the kids send their love. Mama Grace says to tell you to get better. Alvin mopes around the house all the time, making a general nuisance of himself. And," her voice dropped to a softer tone, "you can read the rest of the messages later." The tape slipped from her fingers as she bent down and kissed him gently. "I missed you too."

Mike groaned and wrapped his arms about her. "Oh, Megan, I've missed you so much. You can't know just how much." Desperation filled his voice. "I've never felt so alone as I did after you left." Somewhere behind her, Megan heard Mike's mother excuse herself and leave the room.

They talked, sharing humorous anecdotes that had occurred since they'd last seen one another. As the midwinter sun sank in the western sky, their conversation drifted to spiritual things. Mike's attitude was just as his mother had predicted. He quoted all the right texts, recited all the right clichés, and maintained an attitude of acceptance and contentment. *Maybe Susan is wrong,* she thought to herself. *Maybe Mike's positive, upbeat attitude is genuine. Maybe he's worked his way through this.*

Toward the end of the evening visiting hours, Susan returned. Megan could hardly believe the hours had passed so quickly. Susan invited Megan to spend the Sabbath at home in Glens Falls with Wil and their daughter Kim, but Mike disagreed.

"Uh, I'd rather you stayed with Evelyn," he said unsteadily. "I mean, if you don't mind." Then he brightened. "That way Mom wouldn't have to make the trip to bring you down tomorrow. She can stay home and get some rest herself." Susan shot Megan a tight glance.

"Uh, sure," Megan said carefully.

"I'm glad to hear you're looking out for me," Susan said sarcastically, regaining her usual good nature. "But coming down here is no bother." A look of anxiety flashed in Mike's eyes. Susan smiled. "But then, your father wouldn't mind some relief from his own cooking every now and then. That's a good idea, Michael. I'll take you up on it."

"Then we can talk some more tomorrow, OK?" Megan squeezed his hand.

"I'm counting on it," Mike responded.

After saying goodbye, the two women walked from the room. "Your visit has really boosted his spirits," Susan admitted, "more than I could have imagined."

"Oh, Susan, I hope you didn't feel bad about what Mike said about you staying home tomorrow. Just a short time earlier he told me how tired you must be making the drive down here every day. He wanted to give you a break."

"Well, I have to admit, I did feel a pang of jealousy." She smiled at Megan and continued walking toward the elevators. "It's natural for a mother to feel just a little sorry for herself when another woman comes into her son's life even in the best of circumstances." She reached out and pressed the elevator call button.

"Oh, no, it's not like that—" Megan squirmed.

"Really?" The arrival of the elevator rescued Megan from the moment of truth. They descended to the hospital's parking garage in silence. They stepped from the elevator and the doors closed behind them. Susan waved goodbye, promising to see Megan on Sunday morning before she left for the city. Megan hurried toward her rental car.

Worry gnawed at her mind as she drove to Evelyn's house. Susan's words challenged her thinking. Was there more to Megan's feelings for Mike than simple friendship? Was she falling in love with him? She always enjoyed being with Mike. If things had kept going as they were before the accident, then maybe she could see it. Now everything had gotten so complicated. Now she just didn't know.

Megan slept fitfully that night. Seeing Mike again brought back so many memories; the good times, the accident, the days and nights of pain. When the clock read 4:30 a.m., she gave up trying. She sat up and turned on the light beside her bed. Taking her Bible off the nightstand, she flipped idly through the well-marked pages. She stopped at Psalm 37:4-5.

"Delight yourself in the Lord and He will give you the desires of your heart. Commit your way to the Lord; trust in Him and He will do this: He will make your righteousness shine like the dawn, and the justice of your cause like the noonday sun."

It sounds so simple, Lord, she prayed. *How can Mike's paralysis be a desire of his heart or mine? So simple—just trust, trust . . .* Her mind wandered as she closed her eyes. She awoke at dawn to discover the table lamp still on and her open Bible resting on her chest.

Megan attended church with Evelyn. After a quick lunch, she hurried to the hospital. Mike and Megan spent the afternoon laughing and talking. The only awkward moments came from the mention of Mike's paralysis or the future.

The local minister and his wife stopped in for a visit near sunset. Mike introduced Megan. They talked for a while of Mike's progress. As the middle-aged couple prepared to leave, the minister confided, "You've got a great guy there, young lady. He's gonna' go far with the right woman by his side."

Megan smiled and blushed. "I couldn't agree more, Pastor. Mike is a terrific person." She glanced at Mike. A gray pallor spread across his face. He frowned. When the door closed behind the pastor, Megan suggested having a short worship together to end the Sabbath hours. She had just finished praying when a nurse popped in to announce the end of afternoon visiting hours. Megan bent down and kissed him goodbye, promising to return later in the evening. "You aren't too tired, are you? For me to return?"

Mike leaned his head back against the pillow and closed his eyes. "I am pretty tired. You wouldn't be insulted, would you?"

She shook her head. "Now don't you worry. I'll spend the evening with Evelyn and let you rest. Then, tomorrow, before I head back to the City, I'll stop in for a few minutes, OK?" He nodded and turned his face away as Megan left the room.

Nurses' aids had begun delivering supper trays by the time she reached the elevator. *What had changed Mike so quickly?* Megan wondered. *Within seconds, the laughing, teasing friend I'd enjoyed all afternoon transformed into a tight-lipped, angry stranger. So this is what Susan meant,* she thought. *I guess I've just had my first peek behind that mask. I don't know if the revelation is good or bad.*

She spent another night wrestling with herself. She tried to pray. All she could think of was the fact that in one devastating moment her future had been altered forever. Mike's rejection left her feeling so cold, so empty, so totally alone. She remembered the promise of Hebrews 13, "I will never leave you, nor forsake you." The words sounded hollow to her.

With only a few hours of sleep, Megan headed back to the hospital. The instant she entered Mike's hospital room, she sensed that his attitude had worsened during the night. He looked like he hadn't slept at all. She pasted on a grin and sauntered over to his side.

"Hi, handsome, how ya' feelin'?" Instead of answering, he turned his face toward the window.

"Well, I'm all packed and ready to head to the bus depot." She bent down and kissed his cheek. "You know, that Corsica I rented is a great little car. I've been thinking of buying one of my own. That would make my trips to Albany more pleasant—"

Mike snapped his head around; his eyes narrowed to slits. "What trips to Albany? There can't be any more visits, you know." His fingers tapped out a coded message of impatience on the bed railing. "Can't you get it through your head? I tried to tell you the day you checked out of the hospital. There can be no future for us—you and me. There is no us!"

Megan stepped back as if to avoid his anger. Her eyes smarted with tears. "Mike, I-I-I didn't mean to imply—"

He shook his head wildly. "Can't you understand? God has taken me out of the game during the first quarter. You have the whole game ahead of you." Her eyes telegraphed her confusion. "I was trying to make an analogy but I guess it didn't help!" he snarled and glared at the ceiling.

"I do know a little football, Mike," she snapped back, electrified by his sarcasm. "I had a life before you, you know!"

"That's just the point!" he shouted, not caring that his voice carried beyond the room. "And you have a life after me, Megan. Mine is—is—is"—he searched for his thoughts—"is a dead-end street. You are a beautiful and sensuous woman. You have a future. I don't!"

"Michael, we've been through this before, remember?" She placed her hand on his arm. He snapped away from her touch. His face pinched with pain.

"Then you should have known better than to show up here this weekend in your satiny red dress!"

"Silk," she muttered, clamping her lips tightly together. He glanced at her questioningly. "The red dress is made of silk not satin! And what does my dress have to do with anything?"

"You really don't know, do you?" he snarled and gritted his teeth. "Didn't the friendly little minister's remarks give you any clues?"

"No, I don't understand any of this!" She wrapped her arms about herself and strolled across to the window. "You and I are friends, or at least that's what I thought we were." She blinked back her tears. *I won't cry! I won't cry!*

No one spoke. Beyond the room, the familiar hospital sounds, the service bells, the drone of the intercom, squeeky wheels on carts and gurneys moving up and down the hall clattered on. Inside the room was a deafening barrier of silence.

Megan walked slowly to his bedside. She took his hand in hers and stared into his eyes. "Mike, do you really want me to go away and not come back? Is that what you really, truly want?" He returned her gaze. A haunting sadness filled his eyes. With her fingertip, she drew circles on the back of his hand. "I don't want to make your life more complicated than it all ready is. I care for you too much to allow that to happen—much too much."

Tears welled up in his eyes. He bit his lip and groaned. "That's the problem, Megan. I can't allow myself to fall in love with you any more than I already have. Not now, not ever."

Megan's throat tightened. For a moment she stood silently. "Look," she said finally, "let's not make any hasty decisions, OK? During the next few weeks, we'll pray about our relationship and give God time to lead us."

At the mention of the word prayer, he looked away.

She ran the back of her free hand along the side of his face. "OK?"

"You just don't get it, do you?" He turned back and glared at her in exasperation. "I've had plenty of time to think this through. I don't need more time!" He snatched his hand out of hers. Seconds ticked by like hours.

"Then-then I guess there's not much else to say, huh?" Megan said mechanically. "I'll, uh, just be going then. I have a long drive back to New York." She inched toward the door, staring at the stranger before her. The tears threatening to spill from her eyes forced her to bolt out of the room, straight into Susan.

"What?" The woman caught the disorientated Megan by the shoulders. "What's happening?"

"I-I — ask your son!" Megan broke free and ran to the elevators. She glanced over her shoulder. Susan started to follow after her, a look of concern on her face. Then she turned back to Mike's room.

Megan slammed the palm of her hand against the elevator call button. The doors opened and two white-cloaked men stepped out. One smiled and greeted Megan with a friendly gesture. Megan held her eyes dead center, refusing to connect with anyone. She stepped into the elevator, maintaining her mask of defensive calm until the doors closed. Humiliation, anger, and pain flooded over her as the elevator lurched toward the parking garage.

Like a commander after battle, she counted her losses. Her mother, Alan, and now, Michael. Even her father had built a new life for himself with Libby. Alone? Yes, alone. It was as if the fragile layers of her life had been peeled away like onionskins until there was nothing left. Alone—where would it all end?

C H A P T E R

11

It was early spring. In the outside world, the barren trees of the city sprouted buds. Song birds were returning from their long winter retreat south. Dormant crocus bulbs along Mama Grace's front walk defied the cold, frozen earth and burst forth in tones of lavender, purple, and sunshine yellow. Neighbors, bundled in overcoats, scarves, and wool caps all winter, were enjoying the warmth, taking the time to smile and wave to one another. Yet a winter of doubt had settled on Megan, which no amount of sunshine could thaw. Chilling winds of doubt lashed her heart. Icy storms of anger tore through her soul. Inside, temperatures dropped, threatening to freeze out any sense of peace that might remain.

While Megan received no direct communication from Mike, Susan wrote regularly regarding his progress. "The doctors and his physical therapist are excited about his determination. Sometimes he's so intense, he scares me. What if he never does walk again? What will it do to him?" Each letter ended with an open invitation. "Feel free to visit us anytime." Megan answered his mother's letters, though never making reference to the invitation.

Mama Grace chided Megan for spending her evenings grading papers and workbooks. Sara tried to lure her out on trips to the art galleries and concerts. Megan's father called every week and Libby wrote letters inquiring if all was well. Yet no one could get through. Food tasted like sawdust in her mouth. Her days stretched out in a numbing procession. Megan lived for nighttime when she could escape into the oblivion of sleep, only to awaken with little or no energy to face the new day. She craved isolation, spending as much free time as possible at the public library. At school, the children tiptoed about the classroom, uncertain as to why the happy loving woman had become so distant.

One day her precocious first grader inched up beside her during a study period. "Miss Megan?" Dina's big brown eyes gazed soulfully into Megan's. "Don't you like us anymore?"

Megan dropped the pencil on her desk and stared in surprise at the young child. "Why Dina, I love you very much."

The little girl fidgeted nervously. "Well, you're always grumpy and you don't laugh like you used to or cuddle us when we get hurt or tickle us or . . ."

Megan squeezed her eyes shut as she pulled the child into her arms. What could she say? The little girl was right. Megan suddenly realized she'd been punishing everyone else for Mike's rejection. "Oh, Dina, I'm so sorry. Will you forgive me?"

The little girl's eyes brightened. Her face a beaming smile. "Oh yes, Miss Megan. Oh yes!"

Dina's childlike simplicity goaded Megan's conscience like nothing else could. *You've got to beat this,* an inner voice told her. *Start by putting one foot in front of the other. Even if it's only a baby step, anything's better than losing by default.* By the time Megan left school that afternoon she was determined to get her life back in order—if only she knew where to begin. She didn't know that Mama Grace had already started.

Megan had just closed the front door behind her and was headed up the stairs when Mama Grace called her into the kitchen. Megan popped her head around the doorjamb. "What's up, Mama Grace?"

Mama Grace leaned against the butcher-block island in the middle of her oversized kitchen, up to her elbows in flour and bread dough. "I've got a little job for you, if you don't mind."

Megan licked her lips at the thought of Mama Grace's homemade bread. She set her stack of third- and fourth-grade reading workbooks on the kitchen counter and hurried to the sink. "Just let me wash up and I'll give you a hand."

"Oh, no, I can manage the bread dough just fine. I'm needing help on something else." Mama Grace swiped at a lock of flyaway hair with her forearm. "As you know, tonight is Sara's and my volunteer night at the community center." Megan eyed her suspiciously. Mama Grace pounded away at the pasty lump before her. "Sara came home from work early today with a sore throat and a slight fever. Of course, I sent her right to bed. With Sara sick, I need someone to fill in for her at the center. I was hoping you might give it a shot."

"Hey, wait a minute," Megan interrupted, wagging her head back and forth. "I don't know anything about psychology."

"You don't need to. All you have to do is moderate at a group therapy meeting. The class will do the rest." Mama Grace picked up a knife and expertly sliced the dough into four parts. "It's a grief recovery class."

"But I don't know anything about grief recovery."

"Heaven help us, child." Mama Grace stopped and looked at Megan. "If anyone knows how to deal with grief, you should. First your mom, then Alan, Mike—you've had your share."

"I don't know."

"I really need your help." A firmness entered Mama Grace's voice, one that defied excuses. "My group on single parenting meets at the same time or I'd do it myself."

How could she not do it? No one could ever say no to Mama Grace, at least so it seemed. The woman gave so much to other people and asked for so little in return. Now it was Megan's turn. Reluctantly, she agreed. "Once—just this once!"

Megan scooped up her books and climbed the stairs. She tiptoed into the room and discovered Sara asleep. Megan set her books on the desk. *Now, about turning my life around,* she thought. *I could sure use some exercise. Maybe that's a first step.* She changed clothes and went looking for Alvin. He was in his room doing homework.

"Feel like a quick run around the block?" Megan asked.

"Sure!" Alvin jumped up, happy to escape his math assignment for a few minutes. "I like jogging."

"Me too," Megan nodded. "But I haven't felt much like roaming the city streets alone."

"Anytime you want to go, just call." Alvin stood up straight. "I can take care of you."

Megan laughed. "Thanks Alvin. A girl wouldn't need to worry with you around." The boy smiled.

Out on the sidewalk, they quickly established a comfortable pace. Ribbons of sweat coursed down Megan's back between her shoulder blades sending a sweet warmth through her limbs. After three laps around the block, Megan begged Alvin to stop.

"I've got to rest," she gasped. "Just for a minute." She dropped to a porch step. Alvin joined her.

"You miss him too, don't you?"

Megan stopped short. For a moment she wanted to pretend ignorance, then decided against it. Mike had been a surrogate father and older brother to the boy. If anyone could understand her loneliness, Alvin could. "Yes, I do."

"You gonna' go see him again? The last letter Mike wrote he said he was going home, back to Glens Falls, at the end of the month."

Megan shook her head. Her eyes misted. *He writes to Alvin, but not to me. If it weren't for Susan's letters, I wouldn't know anything about him,* Megan thought. She sighed, "I honestly don't know, Alvin."

"Well," the boy paused and swallowed hard, gathering up his courage. "If you do, do you think I could go along? I'd pay my own way, of course."

"Sure, Alvin. I'd love the company." Megan rose to her feet and stretched.

"Great! That's just great!" Alvin leaped up and started jogging in place, a big grin on his face. "Ready to do a few more laps?"

"Sure. So I ache in the morning—so what?" They finished their workout in time to shower before supper.

During the subway ride to the community center that evening, Megan questioned her wisdom of getting roped into such an unlikely situation. She and Mama Grace arrived at the community center 15 minutes before the meetings were to start. Mama Grace took her to the classroom where the grief recovery group met. The circle of empty chairs sent a jolt of fear through Megan. *I don't belong here,* she thought.

"Now don't be nervous." Mama Grace patted her arm. "Just introduce yourself, tell them that Sara has the flu, then a little about yourself. You'll have an assistant—unofficially, of course," Mama Grace added, "His name is Ken. You'll like him. If anything happens, he'll know what to do. But let me warn you he has a wierd sense of humor."

Megan slumped into one of the chairs and ran her fingers through her hair. "How did you ever get into this, Mama Grace?"

The older woman's eyes clouded. "My husband left me when I was pregnant with my third child, Roxanne. My son, Roland, was barely four at the time, and my daughter Lisa was two. I was a 20-year-old mother with three children to raise and not even a high school diploma."

"How did you manage?"

Mama Grace gazed about the circle of chairs. "To start with, I attended a class like this one."

"But you went back to school, too."

"The class was pretty positive about that," she said. "If they hadn't pushed it so, I doubt I would have had the courage to try."

The woman moved about the circle, straightening and adjusting each chair as she went. "I took in other people's children during the day and studied for my GEDs — high school equivalency test — then took night classes at the community college and later at City College. When I applied for graduate school, I got lucky and won a scholarship."

Megan chuckled. "I'll bet luck had little to do with it."

Mama Grace shrugged. "Anyway, after earning my masters, I worked for Children's Services. It tore me apart each day to see all those kids nobody wanted and watch them fall between the cracks. Then one day I decided I would rather bring these kids into my home and fill their lives with love than to go to a dirty little office each day to collate, stamp, bend, fold, and mutilate them through the system."

Megan arose from the chair and walked across the room to the blackboard. She felt a profound admiration for the woman. "And as if that wasn't enough, you volunteer your time here at the center a couple nights a week."

The older woman's eyes sparkled. "Hey, I get a whole lot more from these people than I could ever give. Love is like that, you know."

"Speaking of love, would you ever marry again?" While she tried to keep her tone light, Megan desperately wanted to hear her answer.

Mama Grace wrinkled her nose and pointed toward the doorway. "Oh, your assistant is here. Megan, meet Ken Savage. Megan is subbing for Sara tonight."

Megan turned around and extended her hand. "Nice to meet you, Mr. — " She was startled to find herself looking down at a man sitting in a wheelchair, his hands resting uselessly by his side.

"Savage," Ken repeated. "Ken Savage." His eyes sparkled and his cocoa-brown face broadened into a grin. An impish set of dimples made him look more like a mischievous 5-year-old than a man on the far side of 40. "Sorry about the handshake. Will a wink do?" he chuckled.

"Ken is a quadriplegic," Mama Grace explained. "It happened in Vietnam, a week before the war ended." Mama Grace walked up behind the man, placed her hands on his shoulders and kissed the top of his head. "This guy is the community center's secret weapon against depression. He's here every evening doing whatever is needed, from telling stories in the nursery to manning a teen hotline."

"I only hang out at the center to be near Gracie Baby, here." Ken joked good-naturedly. "She's one lion of a woman, I can tell you."

Mama Grace huffed and cuffed him on the side of the neck. "Look here, Ken Savage, I am nobody's baby!"

He grinned up at her and attempted his best Irish brogue. "Aw, come on, lass, ye'll break a young man's heart."

"Hmmph! I've got to get to my class." She patted his shoulder and headed out the door.

It didn't take long for the 17 chairs in Megan's class to fill. Ken introduced Megan to the group and started the class discussion. Megan listened as each person shared his feelings and problems.

Harry, a gnarled old gentleman with a shock of thick white hair, told the group about the trouble the welfare agency gave him that week. He had tried to sign up his wife, who suffers from Altzheimers' disease, for Medicare. "They only care about their precious paperwork," he complained.

A plump, middle-aged woman named Evie was concerned for her oldest boy, 12 years old and autistic. She absently picked at a tissue while asking advice on whether or not to place him in a state home or continue to try to raise him herself. She self-consciously touched her black eye and bruised cheek with her hand. "He's already so much stronger than I am. I don't know how much longer I can manage him alone."

One member, Jeff, reminded Megan of Alan. He wore the same image of success, right down to his carefully styled hair and manicured nails. Jeff's brother had recently died of AIDS. "I never imagined that it would happen to anyone I knew," he admitted, "much less my own brother."

Throughout the session, Megan couldn't help noticing a young woman, not much older than herself, who seemed to keep her distance from the group. The woman's skin and hair were perfect. She was wearing an expensive imported wool suit and snakeskin pumps. To Megan, she was the picture of high-class sophistication. Yet the woman was obviously troubled. She stared off into space while the others related their stories. A stripe of rouge blazed against the delicate features of her milky-white cheek. Harsh blue veins pulsated at her temples.

When her turn arrived to speak, she introduced herself as Corrine. In heartwrenching agony, the woman told of hideous physical and sexual abuse inflicted by her own father. The nightmare started for Corrine at the age of 7, when her mother ran off with another man, and lasted until she was 14. As Corrine talked, Megan called up an image

113

of her own father. *Kind, gentle daddy,* she thought. *How lucky I am!*

Corrine smoothed imaginary wrinkles from her suit skirt with painful deliberation. She folded her hands in a tight ball and crossed her slender legs. "You just can't imagine how terrible it was for me all those years."

"Corrine!" Evie's shrill voice cut through the numbing atmosphere pervading the group. "You've suffered things no child should ever have to endure, I admit." She paused and gestured toward the other members of the group. "But we have listened to these same horrid tales week after week. What do you want, a medal? Look around you, we've all suffered."

Megan gasped at Evie's harsh words. What should she do as group leader? She shot Ken a plea for help. A slight shake of his head and the serious look in his eyes told her not to interfere.

"I don't know about the rest of you, but I get sick of hearing her wallow in self-pity every week," Evie continued, her voice climbing to a tantrum-level alert. "As I see it, Corrine, you have a choice. You can live with your sorrow for the rest of your life—build a monument to your pain—or you can put it away and get on with living."

Corrine extended her arm and pointed a single red talon in Evie's direction. Her hand quivered with rage; her face distorted with hate. She opened her mouth to speak, but no words came out. When she finally found her voice, it curled into a whine. "I don't have to listen to this! I came here for support, not to be insulted."

"Wait a minute," Ken boomed. "May I speak?" Corrine nodded, her lower lip quivering. "As you know, Evie, there is no set time schedule to the healing process. We all walk that road alone and deal with it in our own ways. The purpose of this group is to be Corrine's support system, to love her unconditionally as God loves her and grieves with her—no matter how long it takes." Corrine adopted a look of righteous indignation, extracted an Irish lace-edged linen handkerchief from her purse and dabbed her eyes. Evie stared at the floor as Ken continued speaking. "On the other hand, Corrine, Evie is right too. Sooner or later, you have to choose to move on. I know it's a stupid cliché, but today can be the first day of the rest of your life, if you choose to let it."

"Listen to him, Corrine. He's been there." Everyone turned to look at the wizened Oriental woman sitting silently just near the door to the hallway. The woman had been so silent, Megan barely noticed her presence. "I remember when Ken returned from Vietnam. He had nothing. His own parents were embarrassed by him." Ken didn't say anything. "On top of his injury, he had to deal with the guilt of having killed innocent people in the line of duty."

Ken lifted his eyes toward the old woman. "I remember also, Grandma Lin, while lying helpless in an iron lung, not even able to control my own breathing let alone my destiny, I composed a list in my mind. In one column, I listed my reasons for living, and in the other much longer one, my reasons for wanting to die. The two columns fought furiously every day for more than a year." The gentle purr of his motorized wheelchair could be heard as Ken crossed the room to face Corrine. Megan sensed that if he could have, he would have reached out and unfolded the woman's tight little fists. "One day a friend shared a quotation from Ernest Hemingway's *Farewell to Arms* with me. He said, 'The world breaks everyone, but some become strong in the broken places.' Too bad he didn't take his own advice to heart. Corrine, you and everyone here needs to become strong in the broken places."

"The best way to heal from a tragedy is to help someone else," Grandma Lin added.

"Right on, Grandma!" Ken's face brightened. "Corrine, have you ever thought of volunteering to work on the rape crisis line one night a week?" The group burst into laughter.

"Ken is famous for his recruitment methods," Grandma Lin chuckled. "Nobody escapes his persuasive grip."

He shook his head and grinned. "Well, maybe. But I'm being serious here. Who can better understand the devastation of rape than someone who's been through it?" Corrine nodded slowly.

"I'll think about it," she said softly. "That's all I'll promise for now."

Ken turned his chair to face Evie. "I suspect you're hurting more tonight than you've let on to us. Do you want to talk about it?"

Trembling, her fists clenched and her mouth drawn into a pinched seam, Evie shook her head. "Not yet," she whispered. A buzzer announced the end of the groups evening session. The group began to break up. In a few minutes only Ken and Megan were left in the empty room.

"Grandma Lin seems to be a very wise woman," Megan wondered. "Is she here as a volunteer too?"

"Yes and no," Ken said. "Her wisdom comes from suffering also. She escaped from Cambodia after seeing her husband and five children slaughtered by one of Pol Pot's death squads." Ken sighed. He closed his eyes for a moment, then looked at Megan. "Grandma Lin and I have seen every problem imaginable come through those doors during the last 15 years. And, just when you think you've heard the worst, another even more grisly tale is told."

Megan arose from her chair and slipped her arms into her jean jacket. "It kind of makes you put your own problems into perspective, doesn't it?"

He studied her face intensely. "Sometimes. But grief is grief; pain is pain. People go through the same healing process whether one suffers from a job loss, rejection from a lover, or death in the family." He lifted one eyebrow and continued searching her face for information.

She busied herself straightening the chairs in the circle. "I never knew that."

"Most people don't."

She stopped a moment and frowned. "I can't say I enjoyed tonight, but I am glad I came. You've given me lots to think about, Ken."

"Well, I hope your first visit won't be your last." He whirled his chair about and headed for the doorway. "Why don't you come on down to the pressure cooker with me until Mama Grace finishes with her group? She always runs overtime."

"The pressure cooker?"

"Yeah, the crisis line phone room." Megan walked beside his chair as he explained. "Each of the four corners of the room houses a separate crisis center—for the family, the teen, rape, and last, suicide. I bet you'd be great working one of the teen lines."

She chuckled deep in her throat and cast him a sidelong smirk. "Grandma Lin was right. You never do quit, do you?"

An imitation of shame and guilt spread across his face, then he winked. "Hey, what can I say?" A devilish grin spread across his face. "I'm a native New Yorker. We're too tough to quit!"

CHAPTER

12

Circles, hearts, daisies, and cubes. Megan doodled on the pad of paper in front of her. She wrote out her name in Old English script, outlining the M with flourishes and trellis work. She absently hummed a favorite tune. After four weeks of training for the volunteer teen hot line, she found herself enjoying the task more each night she worked. The problems varied anywhere from "how can I get my little brother to stay out of my room" to "my mom and dad are getting a divorce and I feel all alone."

Mostly, Megan's instructor had taught her how to listen without making judgments and how to get through the surface to the underlying problem. Helping other people with their problems gave her insights into her own discouragment. Talking with Ken, before and after their shifts, helped her understand Mike better also.

Suddenly the phone rang. "Teen Hotline, this is Megan. May I help you?"

At first no one replied.

"Hello? Is anyone there?" Megan tried again. "Can I help you?"

"Uh, yeah," a tentative voice responded. "I think so, anyway." It was a young man, maybe 18. He hesitated. "I don't know why I'm calling you or what I'm supposed to say."

"Why don't you begin with your name." Megan's pencil traced lazy figure eights on the scratch pad. The Monday night calls were seldom as plentiful or as serious as on other nights of the week.

"I don't know if that's a good idea. I don't know if any of this is a good idea really—"

"It's no big deal," Megan soothed. She could sense tension in his voice. "You don't have to give me your real name. I just need to be able

to call you something—Jerry, Ebenezer, Oxnard—anything will do."
Again the caller hesitated.

"Call me Jed."

"Ok, Jed." She sighed with relief. "What would you like to talk about?" The silence that followed this question lasted so long she feared her young caller had hung up.

"I think I might have done a very stupid thing."

"What did you do that was so stupid?"

"I don't know where to start. There's this girl named Gina. I've been dating her for two weeks now." Jed paused between each sentence. "At school today a couple of guys told me that she had only dated me on a dare. When I asked her about it, she laughed at me—right in my face. And she admitted that she and her friends had been playing a game called 'Truth or Dare' at a slumber party and—" His voice cracked with emotion. "And I was her dare. She said I was the class nerd and that she had to date me for two weeks!"

Megan seethed at the thought of how cruel this unfeeling girl had been to so cruelly trample this boy's confidence and self-esteem. "Oh Jed, I'm sorry."

"Oh, don't feel sorry for me. I'm used to that sort of stuff. It's just that I didn't expect it from Gina, I guess." The pain in his voice made Megan wince. He continued. "But that's not why I called. I-I-I, uh, well when I got home from school, I found some pills in my mom's night-stand and I . . . " his voice trailed off.

"Jed? Hey, Jed, are you there?" Megan straightened in her chair. She signaled to Ken who was at the telephone station beside her and scribbled him a note: "Help! Suicide attempt. I can't do this!"

"I took 'em all!" Jed was back again. "I wanted Gina and her friends to feel sorry for what they'd done. Now I'm scared."

"Jed, can you tell me what kind of pills you took?"

"Valium, I think."

"Valium?" Megan repeated. She wanted to be sure she heard him correctly. "Is that what you swallowed, Jed? Valium?"

"Yeah, that's right," he said. "I've got the bottle right here."

The other members of the crisis team gathered about Megan's station. Vera, a trained psychologist and the team leader, placed a note in front of Megan. "How many and when?" Megan nodded.

"Jed? Do you know how many you swallowed?"

"I dunno'—15 or so, I guess—"

"How long ago? Ten minutes, an hour?" Megan leaned her elbows on the desktop.

"I don't know," he sounded listless. "A while ago."

"Where are you, Jed? Where do you live?" Megan continued questioning the boy. The team leader dashed across the room to another telephone extension and placed an emergency call to 911.

"Look, it's not important." Jed was beginning to get exasperated. "It's too late anyway." Each of his words slid into the next. "Look, I gotta' go."

Vera flashed another sign in front of Megan's face. "Keep him talking. Police tracing call."

Again Megan nodded. She forced herself to maintain a calm, smooth tone. "Jed, listen. It doesn't have to be too late. Just tell me where you are. I can send help." A hush fell over the group as Vera pressed a red button on the telephone console allowing Jed's side of the conversation to be heard in the room.

"No, no. It's too late now."

Megan tried another tactic. "Are you alone? Is there anyone you would like me to call?"

"Naw, Mom's at work. I better go."

"How about your dad? Is he there?"

A static tension filled the room as they awaited the boy's reply. "On my fifth birthday, my dad went to the corner grocery store for ice cream and never came back."

"Oh," Megan paused to regroup her thoughts. "Jed, you still haven't answered most of my questions. How many pills did you take?"

"I told you—15 or so . . ."

"OK, I got it now," she assured him. "I don't remember, did you tell me when you took them?"

"I dunno. I gotta go." The boy yawned into the telephone receiver. "I feel so sleepy . . ."

Megan's heart raced in frustration. How could she keep this boy talking until help arrived? She changed tactics. "Is this Gina really worth dying for? She sounds like a real jerk."

"Oh, no, you got it all wrong," he insisted. "I'm the jerk. Gina's hot stuff."

"She doesn't sound it to me." Megan waited, but no response came. "Jed? Jed!"

"Yeah, yeah, I hear you," he mumbled. "You just wouldn't understand what it's like to be made a fool of in front of the entire school."

"Oh, really? You'd be surprised how much I do understand." She paused to scan the sea of concerned faces surrounding her. "Jed, I haven't told many people this, but I do understand how you feel. This Christmas, I was supposed to be married to Alan, whom I thought was the neatest guy in the world. Last summer he dumped me. Rejection really hurts, huh?"

"Big deal—so you understand, but you don't care. No one does." The boy's slur became more pronounced with each passing minute. Megan's heart pounded in her ears. Sweat beaded across her brow.

"You're wrong, Jed. I really do care. And what about your mom? I'm sure she cares."

"Are you kidding? She hardly knows I'm alive. She'd love to be rid of me." His voice was full of hate. Megan listened as Jed described his family life, his constant humiliation at school, and his feelings of uselessness. Five, ten, fifteen minutes passed. Especially bitter were his memories of his classmates' ridicule.

"We've all been hurt at one time or another," Megan reasoned. "By stupid, ignorant people like Gina and like my boyfriend. That's life, unfortunately. But you don't have to give up."

As he kept talking, the faint sound of a siren wailing in the distance came over the phone. It grew louder and louder. A few moments later the sound of insistent pounding on a door could be heard.

"Jed, go open the door. Someone's there who can help you."

She heard a groan, followed by the scraping of a chair leg on a wooden floor. An adult male voice came on the line, "Good job, Megan. The cavalry's arrived. We'll take over now."

A cheer of victory filled the phone room. Megan slumped down in her chair like a rag doll.

Ken winked at her and shouted above the din. "Whoa! Chalk one up for the good guys!"

Vera came up and gave Megan a big squeeze. "You did fine, Megan."

"I thought you'd take over when I told you how serious the problem was."

Vera shook her head. "No, I was afraid he'd hang up if you didn't stick with him. He was skittish already."

A shudder passed through Megan. She clutched her arms and shivered, "I felt so helpless."

Vera gave her a second squeeze. "Welcome to the club."

News of the aborted suicide rocketed through the community center at warp speed. When she left for home that night, Megan staggered through a guantlet of goodwill from the center's staff and volunteers. All she could think of was how good a hot shower and clean sheets were going to feel. She'd never felt so tired, yet so supercharged in her entire life.

How wonderfully fragile the gift of life truly is, she thought, as the hot spray of the shower pelted her shoulders and back. *And today one hurting, insecure teenager chose to hold onto that gift a little longer. I can't believe it. I've got to tell someone! But who would understand how I feel? Mike! He'd understand, or at least, the old Mike would.*

When everyone retired for the night, she tiptoed downstairs to the kitchen table and composed a letter to him—her first in months. She told him about the people she'd met at the community center, about Ken and his irresistible good humor, about Mama Grace's incredible courage, and about her newest friend, Jed.

"Tonight Jed helped me discover a purpose to the pain in a Christian's life," she wrote. "First, that pain tells me I'm still alive regardless of life's tragedies—that I'm a survivor. Second, my pain makes it possible for me to reach out to someone else who is hurting. Because I have suffered from rejection and loneliness, I can feel another's pain.

"I never understood God's promises," she continued writing. "Both Mama Grace and Ken have helped me see Him less as a grandpa and more as a fellow sufferer. I never realized how immature my views of God and His obligations to me were. They've helped me grow."

Megan thought about the boy who touched her heart that night. She tried to imagine what it must have been like for the 5-year-old boy waiting for his daddy to bring home the ice cream for the birthday party—waiting for a man who never returned.

"How can Jed ever accept the constant love of his Heavenly Father when his earthly father betrayed him so?" she wrote. "You and I are so lucky to have Dads who exemplify God's love. Perhaps it's that human bond of love that gives our lives the necessary tensile strength for survival. As for Gina"—Megan stabbed at the words—"I'd like to get my hands on her! If only she knew how thoughtless and cruel her little game was, she might not be so happy-go-lucky with others' feelings next time.

"Mike," she concluded, "please forgive me for allowing my pride to keep me from writing before. I once vowed to be your friend. If you'll let me, I want to keep that vow. I'm not asking for your love, just your friendship." She looked over her words, then signed, "With tender affection, Megan."

She folded the pages carefully and addressed the envelope. Doubts surfaced in her mind. *How will Mike deal with my honesty?* she worried. *With all the honesty his paralysis has forced him to face, will he misinterpret and think I am preaching at him? Maybe I shouldn't leave myself open to rejection again. No, I wrote from my heart as I would to any close friend. If our friendship is going to work, I have to be able to do that,* she decided. With a defiant step she walked to the mailbox by the door and dropped it inside. Suddenly, a wave of relief surged over her. The tonnage she'd been lugging about on her back all winter lightened a bit. She felt light, free of care. Laughter bubbled up inside, releasing a childlike hope buried within.

The next morning was business as usual. She ate her breakfast, grabbed her lunch bag, and rushed out the door. Heavy ash-grey clouds threatened overhead. *What a beautiful day!* she told herself. The squealing brakes, the relentless traffic, and the sea of humanity surging around her became a vibrant symphony of life to her. She walked toward the subway station on the corner, her black leather pumps slapping the concrete sidewalk like determined hands. *Mike needs to know he's not alone,* she argued. *He needs to be reminded that there are other people in the world suffering and coping with their pain—Ken calls them victorious survivors.* A satisfied smile spread across her face. *A victorious survivor—that's me!* She hadn't thought of herself in those terms. "And dear, sweet Mike," she whispered aloud. "Even if you don't know it yet, you are one too."

When she returned home from school that afternoon, a fat manila envelope lay on her bed. It was her acceptance to attend a graduate school in Michigan in the fall. *Life goes on,* she reminded herself, as she dug into the material excitedly.

Later that night, she told her friends at the community center about her decision to return to school. On Thursday, she decided to write to Mike of her good news.

"Ken suggested I attend summer school and get some prerequisites out of the way," she wrote him. "That way I can enter as a full-time graduate student in the fall. Mama Grace has invited me to stay here and attend City College. My dad would prefer I enroll in the summer sessions at the University of New Mexico. I guess the Lord and I have a lot to talk about during the next few weeks."

The next day Megan volunteered to pick up a few grocery items on her way home from school for Mama Grace. By early afternoon she found herself eagerly heading for Brooklyn's famous shopping district: Eighteenth Avenue. Strolling past the open-air markets and tiny shops reminded her of an earlier time—of places and people she'd only read about. When ice wagons rumbled over cobblestones, when kids rolled hoops down the crowded sidewalk, and drivers of Model "A" Fords rattled down the cobbled streets.

A honking car horn brought Megan back to the present. She leaped sideward to avoid colliding with two boys racing by on skateboards. Two weathered grandmas hauled their wire shopping carts past the open stalls on the avenue. One middle-aged woman argued with a scowling clerk over the price of his bell peppers. Sunlight danced on the long red mane of a happy young girl walking with a glowering young man wearing a leather jacket. Harried young mothers, wheeling babies in carriages loaded down with groceries, rushed from shop to shop.

"Hey, lady." Megan was startled by a voice calling from behind her. "Ya' gonna' stand there all day or what?"

"Oh, sorry," she mumbled, backing into a display of golden delicious apples. Three of the yellow fruit tumbled from their shaky perch. Megan was barely able to catch them before they hit the ground. She sighed in relief.

"Hey, watch it, lady," the shopkeeper shouted. "You bruise 'em, you buy 'em."

A large, pleasant-looking woman, standing near the onion bin, smiled at the embarrassed Megan. "Don't worry about him," she said in a voice the shopkeeper couldn't avoid hearing. "At the prices he charges, he can afford a few bruised apples."

Megan smiled gratefully at the woman and hurried down the street to the grocer Mama Grace usually called on. She handed the shopping list to the clerk, and within a few minutes he'd filled the order. She added a bag of homemade bagels to the stack, paid for the items, then jammed everything into Mama Grace's nylon mesh shopping bags. Grabbing the handles of the two bags, she headed back down the street. The warm sunshine and gentle breeze convinced Megan to walk the 20 blocks home instead of riding the subway. At the corner, she bought herself a hot pretzel to eat along the way. She shifted her parcels to her left hand and started walking.

I am really going to miss all of this, she conceded, nibbling as she walked. She'd had hot pretzels before in other places, but none compared to New York's. *The same goes for New York pizza,* she decided.

When Megan thought of pizza, she always thought of Mike. For her, the two would forever go together. She remembered sampling her first pizza slice topped with green olives. How surprised she was to discover she liked it. She laughed out loud when she recalled his critical reaction to pineapple-topped Hawaiian pizza.

"It's an acquired taste," she had told him.

"Not during my lifetime!" He had crossed his eyes for emphasis.

Megan shuddered when a dark cloud passed in front of the sun. "It isn't fair." How many times since the accident had she repeated those three little words—sometimes crying, sometimes shouting, and sometimes in a whisper? Whenever Ken heard her complain, he reminded her that life was not fair, that it never had been and never would be. Megan didn't know Ken's religious affiliation, but she was certain of his rock-solid faith.

"Like it or not, we live out our days in a world of sin. It's not how long we live, or how well we live, but rather, how we choose to live those days that makes the difference."

Megan frowned. "But God promised—"

Ken's dark eyes pierced her through. "God promised He will never leave you, nor forsake you."

And He hadn't, she realized as she hurried home. *Not for a moment.* Sometime during the last 24 hours, it had all come together—Ken's words, her father's words, Mama Grace's, the agonizing months of searching the Bible for answers—all of it. When she lost her mother, Megan had entered a long, painfully dark tunnel. And after three years of mourning her mother, being rejected by Alan, the trauma of the accident, her father's remarriage, falling in love with and then losing Mike, she had emerged into the sunlight once again. She realized that no matter how dark it had gotten down in the bowels of her despair, she'd never been totally alone. God hadn't been waiting at the far end of the tunnel waiting for her to come out. He'd been right there beside her suffering the same pain and emptiness she suffered. Like she had understood Jed's pain, God knew and understood hers.

If only Mike could— She squelched the thought. "Sorry Lord," she prayed, "I'm trying to run ahead of the Holy Spirit, aren't I? In Your time, not mine. You love him more than I ever could."

She paused at the street corner, waiting for the "walk" signal to appear. "Is it time, Lord," she prayed, "that I accept Susan's invitation?"

CHAPTER

13

Megan stopped to enjoy the scent of freshly opened blossoms on a fruit-tree branch, then skipped on down the street. She flung her arms upward, in spite of the grocery bags. "I thank You, Lord, for this most amazing day." Lettuce leaves and celery stalks protruding from the overstuffed grocery bags fluttered to the rhythm of her bouncing walk.

"Hi, I'm home," she called, opening the door into Mama Grace's house. She nudged the door closed with her knee.

"Megan?" Mama Grace called from the kitchen. "You have a long distance telephone call. You wanna' take it in the hall?"

Who would be calling me? she wondered.

Megan set the groceries on the floor and picked up the receiver. "Hello?"

"Hello, Megan?" It was a familiar woman's voice.

"Susan?" A sudden fear swept over her. "Is everything all right? Mike is OK, isn't he?"

"Oh yes, more than fine," the woman explained. "He's making great progress, now that he's home from the hospital. The insurance covered the cost of a custom built van for him—one with hand controls and a wheelchair lift. But I still have to drive him to Albany for treatments. I think he's nervous about driving again."

"I can understand that. I remember how I felt the first time I rode in an automobile after the accident."

"Well, before it came he vowed he'd never drive it. But Kim bugged him until he agreed to give it a try. He's been practicing in the driveway and in the empty field behind the house, but hasn't done any on-the-road driving yet."

Megan leaned against the stairwell. "How's he managing the stairs at home?"

"Wil built a ramp up to the back porch and converted my sewing room next to the kitchen into a bedroom so that Mike doesn't have to maneuver any stairs at all."

She detected a touch of pride in Susan's voice. "Mike is lucky to have you two for parents."

"Well, we do our best, but Arnold and René Harrington really made it all possible. They're Nicky's parents—the driver of the other car," Susan explained. "They're quite wealthy and more importantly, they're Christians. They've become like family to us since the accident and can't do enough for Mike."

Megan thought for a moment. "I think Mr. Harrington called me after the accident to be certain I was doing all right and had everything I needed."

"Probably so. I called to let you know that Mike received your letters. I've caught him reading and rereading them a dozen times over. He really misses you." Susan paused for a moment, then continued. "I know I've asked before, but I was wondering if you could come up for a visit soon."

"I'd love to, Susan." Megan twisted the telephone cord around her fingers and wrist, then untwisted it. "But don't you think that, under the circumstances, it would be best to wait until Mike invites me himself? Maybe after we've exchanged a few letters, established a communication link once again. Can you understand?"

"Yes," the voice on the other end replied, "you're probably right. I know he knows what he wants. I just hope he doesn't let his stupid pride get in the way much longer." Megan imagined the frustrated expression on the fiesty lady's face. "Well, I had to try at least. Have a good weekend, you hear?"

"Goodbye, Susan," Megan said, and hung up the phone. She picked up her grocery bags and took them into the kitchen. She could tell by the expression on Mama Grace's face that the woman was about to explode with curiosity. "Mike's mom wanted to give me an update on his condition."

"And?"

Megan looked at Mama Grace with wide innocent eyes. "And what?" She shoved a bag onto the counter. "Here's your stuff. I hope I got everything you asked for."

Mama Grace glared and growled, then gave her the ultimate compliment. "You did good, kid."

"Thanks." She placed a quick kiss on the woman's cheek and skipped up to her room to clean for Sabbath. Just knowing Mike had cared enough to reread the two letters made her sing.

As she vacuumed the worn gold shag carpet in her room, she sang at the top of her voice. Still charged with energy, she vacuumed out into the hallway, changing outlets as she ran out of cord. When Megan finished vacuuming the entire second floor, she stashed the machine in the hall closet and hurried downstairs.

"OK, I have two ready and willing hands that need to be told what to do," Megan called as she burst into the kitchen. Mama Grace smiled her most knowing smile.

"Here," she handed her a head of lettuce. "Toss a salad around."

After supper, the family remained around the table for evening worship. They were just finishing prayer when the telephone rang.

"I'll get it." Alvin leaped to his feet. He grabbed the receiver from its wall cradle. "Hello? Franklin residence, Alvin speaking."

Megan rubbed her eyes and yawned. *It will feel so good to get into bed tonight,* she thought. Suddenly Alvin's voice broke through her grogginess.

"Mike? Mike! I don't believe it! How ya' doin' man?"

Megan's eyes flew open. She jerked her head around to look at Alvin.

"Yeah, I've missed you too, man. Yeah, yeah, you told me a little about your new wheels in your last letter. Wow, that's cool!"

Mama Grace rose to her feet. "Children, let's get the table cleared and dishes done."

Trying not to eavesdrop on Alvin's side of the conversation, Megan gathered up her dishes and carried them to the sink. One of the girls took the dishes from her hands. "I'll do that Miss Megan. It's my turn to clear tonight."

"A whole week?" Alvin sounded ecstatic. "I'll ask my mom and let you know, OK? Right, you got it, man. I'll call her." Alvin clamped the palm of his hand over the mouthpiece and shouted, "Megan! Mike wants to talk with you."

She tapped the boy on the shoulder and grinned. "Thank you. I'm right here behind you, Alvin. I'll take it in the living room."

She ran down the hallway and into the parlor. Pausing a moment to catch her breath, she picked up the receiver. "Hi."

"Hi, to you too." Mike's familiar voice was cheerful.

"This is a pleasant surprise." Megan held the receiver close to her face as she seated herself on the sofa. "I just talked with your mom this afternoon."

"She told me. She suggested I give you a call."

Megan felt a pang of disappointment. "Oh." She slipped out of her shoes and curled her legs beneath her on the couch.

"I enjoyed your letters," Mike went on. "I've missed hearing from you. My mother keeps me informed, but it's not the same."

"Yeah, I know what you mean. I've missed you too." Nervous, she twisted the cord around her fingers.

The conversation began slowly, hesitantly. But once started, they talked for hours. Sometime during the evening, each of the family members whispered goodnight to her from the hallway, sent their love to Mike, then disappeared upstairs to bed.

In the middle of a discussion of the latest Middle East crisis, Mike abruptly changed the subject. "Please forgive me for acting like a jerk, for sending you away."

Tears formed in her eyes. "I—I understand. It's OK."

"No, it's not OK to take my anger out on you."

"Really, Mike, I do understand. As I said in the second letter, Ken has taught me so much about the healing process. Your behavior was only natural."

"Uh, yeah, right." His voice dropped, though not enough to disguise the sarcasm. "How does he know how I'm supposed to feel? What is he, a shrink?"

She bristled at his tone. "No, he's a quadriplegic."

"A what? What do you have, a fetish for cripples?"

She bit back the nasty retort that leaped to her lips; her nostrils flared with anger. "Cripples? I can't speak for you, Mike, but Ken is light years away from being a cripple, as you put it. For that matter, he is the most all-together guy I've ever met." She took a deep breath. *Uh oh, too far,* she thought. "Sorry, Mike, I had no—"

"So are you two dating or something?" The edge remained in his voice.

"Excuse me?" She laughed. The idea of dating Ken, a man older than her own father, was the furthest thought from her mind.

"Sorry, it's none of my business who you date. This call isn't turning out at all like I planned. I'd better hang up."

Megan lurched forward. "Wait! We can't leave things like this

---

between us." The line went dead. "Well, of all the . . ." She hung up the receiver, turned out the living room lights and hurried upstairs to her room. She stormed into the room.

"He's a jerk, an absolute jerk!" she shouted. "He calls me. He says he misses me. He's in the middle of apologizing to me then, wham, he's insulting me instead. And to top it off, he hangs up on me!"

"Will you keep it down!" Sara grimaced. "You'll wake the whole house." She looked at Megan's reddened face. "I presume you're talking about Mike Feldman."

"Of course I'm talking about Mike Feldman. Who else?" She strode to the window, glanced down at the street, then turned. "Who else? He's the only human being in planet earth that can get me so riled so easily! I don't know why I even care."

"Oh, yes you do. This is Sara you're talking to—your best buddy and confidante," Sara reminded. "And if you stop ranting long enough to think about it—"

"Do you know what he had the audacity to ask? He asked me straight out if I was dating Ken—Ken of all people!" Megan strode across the room again.

"Can't you figure out why he might jump to that conclusion?" Sara smiled. "You must admit that you do mention Ken often in your conversations."

"But I—"

"I know." Sara held up a hand to silence her. "I know you and I know Ken, but Mike doesn't know much about either of you." Sara shook her head. "For a woman so smart, you certainly can be dense."

"I don't understand what—"

"Megan, just listen a minute. Mike loves you, not as a friend and definitely not as a brother. He loves you as a man loves a woman, as Adam loved Eve, as Boaz loved Ruth, as Joseph loved Mary, as Romeo—"

"OK, OK, I got the picture already!" Megan plopped down in the middle of her own bed and curled her legs under her.

"No, I don't think you do. Look at this from Mike's side. He'd just gotten you to respond to his attentions when the accident severed what he believed to be his only chance with you."

"But I . . ."

"Will you let me finish?" Sara interrupted. "At first, all he could think of was his own loss which included being unable to adequately demonstrate his love for you—ever. All this talk about sending you away was actually a declaration of his unselfish love for you. He didn't want you to feel obligated to him. To pity him. Maybe he'd even given up all hope until your letters arrived."

"I only meant to—"

"You meant to do just what you did, admit it. There's nothing wrong with that, Megan. Obviously, you love him too." Sara sat up and adjusted her blankets about her waist. "Your letters gave him hope on one hand and, on the other hand, threw Ken—who Mike has never met, I might add—in his face. His natural feelings of jealousy arose."

Megan hugged a bed pillow to her chest and buried her chin in its softness. "I see what you mean. So where are we now? Where do we go—"

The phone at the foot of the stairs interrupted her sentence. Sara tipped her head toward the door. "I'd suggest that you answer the telephone."

Megan sprang from the bed and raced down the stairs. "Hello?"

"Hi." It was Mike. "Before you exercise your right to hang up on me, I'm sorry. I'm acting stupid and I don't like it."

"I'm sorry too." She leaned against the wall and slid down to a seated position on the floor beside the telephone stand. "I came on pretty strong myself."

"Look, I think it's time we stop playing hide 'n' seek with one another. We need to talk—face to face, I mean. Like adults."

Megan bit her lip and ran her fingers idly through her hair. "I agree. When and where?"

"I know this is short notice, but how about tomorrow at my house? I'd come to New York, but it wouldn't be fair to ask my folks to drive me. They've done enough already."

"I can't," Megan sighed. "I'm supposed to help out at church this weekend. And there's a teen outing to Long Island tomorrow afternoon. But there's always next weekend."

He hesitated for a moment. "Oh, OK, I guess I'll have to be patient." She detected the disappointment in his voice.

"I guess we both will," she admitted.

Mike called her at 8:30 each evening during the days that followed. They talked for hours at a time. The thoughts he'd kept so long bottled up inside burst free. On Thursday evening, he reminded her that he'd purchased her a plane ticket and it was waiting for her at the airport.

"A plane ticket?" Megan was surprised. "Mike, I can't let you buy me a plane ticket. You and your folks don't have money to spread around freely. And what about these phone calls? I love talking with you, but—"

A chuckle came over the lines. "I thought you'd never ask. I've been dying to tell you all week, but I wanted to set you up first."

"I beg your pardon?" She scowled and shook her head. "Tell me what?"

"Money is no object, at least at the moment. The phone calls, your ticket, I paid for it all out of my own earnings. I am a working man now."

"That's wonderful. Your mom didn't mention anything about you—"

"I asked her not to tell you. I wanted to tell you myself." The pride in his voice brought tears to her eyes. "The chaplain at the hospital arranged to have me hired part-time to work especially with the younger patients. So three days a week, when I go in for my own treatments, I put in a few hours helping kids cope with their problems."

"I-I don't know what to say." She blinked back her tears. "I think it's absolutely terrific."

"I've made many of the same discoveries as you have during the past few months. I'd been praying for answers about us and then when I read your letters—wow! It's like God speaking to me directly through you."

Megan wiped her tears on her sleeve. "I've been praying too, Mike."

An aura of reverence filled his voice. "It's like even though we've been apart during the past few months, God has been bringing us together." He chuckled. "Sorry, now I'm being corny."

"No, Mike, that's not corny, it's beautiful." She continued, "God knew you and I needed to heal apart from each other in order to build a strong independent faith in Him. I had to get over so many hurts and learn to trust Him. And you, you had mountains of pain to conquer— pain that I had no way of understanding."

His voice broke. "We have lots to talk about tomorrow night, don't we?"

"Lots and lots," Megan whispered.

CHAPTER

14

Megan dug her fingernails into the padded armrests when the sleek commuter jet screeched and bounced on the surface of the airport runway. *I hate small planes,* she thought as she clenched her fingers nervously. As usual, the other passengers crammed the aisle waiting to get off. She watched them inch by—mostly rumpled, tired-looking businessmen going home for the weekend. Butterflies flitted against her stomach lining when she thought of Mike and their weekend together. Before leaving New York, she'd called her father in New Mexico and told him about Mike and their phone conversations. "I need you to pray for me, Daddy. I feel like this weekend is a major intersection in my life. I'm so scared I'll mess up again."

" 'Lo, I am with you always'—words straight from the Master's lips, precious one," he reminded. "Libby's and my thoughts will be with you all weekend. And, by the way, who says you messed up before? You're a champion, remember that."

Megan loosened her seat belt. She stood up and removed her carry-on case from under the seat in front of her. She grabbed her shoulder bag and coat from the seat before heading down the plane's narrow aisle. She trembled at the thought of seeing Mike again. Were it not for her fear of small planes, she half-wished she could just stay on board and fly back to New York immediately.

Megan emerged from the corridor to an empty waiting lounge and glanced at her watch. The plane had landed 15 minutes early. She walked over to the huge window that overlooked the runways and dropped her travel case beside a chair and sat down. She leaned back and yawned. With the end of the school year approaching she'd been up late every night for two weeks grading workbooks and math papers. She closed her eyes and twisted her head from side to side to ease the nagging pain gripping the back of her neck. Suddenly someone's hand began massaging her neck.

"Oh!" She leaped to her feet and whirled about, her eyes wide with terror. Mike's laughter filled the empty lounge. She pressed her hand on her heart and gasped. "Don't ever sneak up on me like that again. It's a wonder I didn't clobber you with my bag." She picked up her suitcase and handbag. "Maybe I will anyway!"

He threw his hands up in front of his face to defend himself. "No, no, you wouldn't hit a guy in a wheelchair now would you?"

"I would if he deserved it."

He looked up at her through penitent eyes. "I promise I'll try to be good. Do we need to pick up the rest of your luggage?"

"Nope, this is it." Megan gave his wheelchair a once over. "That's quite the jitney you have there."

"It gets me around." Mike gave a quick pull with his strong arms on the slender wheels and whirled the chair around. "I can't do wheelies yet, but I'm working on it. Come on, let's roll." Together they headed toward the airport corridor.

Megan had to step up her pace in order to stay even with him. "So is your mom or dad waiting for us in the car?"

"Be patient woman!" He rolled through the airport terminal's electronic doors into the parking lot. "The big advantage in having one of these," he tapped his chair affectionately, "is I get my own special parking place." He waved his hand dramatically toward a black van with a red and a purple racing stripe down the side. "Behold, the chariot. It's a Ford 150. Their suspension can best take the weight of the lift."

"Mike, it's gorgeous!" Megan gaped at the shiny new vehicle. "But your mom said you didn't want to take it out on the road yet."

He reached for her hand and led her to the van. "That, my dear, was before I knew you were coming for a visit. Look here." He pulled a remote control unit from his pocket and pressed a button. The side doors slid open. He pushed the next button to lower the lift. "Hop aboard. I know how much you enjoy riding elevators." Cautiously she stepped onto the metal lift.

"By the way, that's a genuine, top-of-the-line Ricon lift." The lift carried her to the level of the van floor. "Be sure to duck before you get off and step over, not on, the metal panel. You get the navigator's seat, while I get to be pilot."

She hopped off the lift and into the van. While he lowered the lift again, she ran her hand across the seat and dashboard. "I love it. Can I do anything to help you?"

"Absolutely not. Just buckle up, my love. I can handle this myself." Grinning with obvious delight, he guided his chair onto the lift and rode it to the top. Once inside the vehicle, he pressed the button to close the double doors. With the help of metal crutches, he lifted himself into the swivel driver's seat. "I could have had the driver's seat removed but it's safer to use a regular bucket seat than a wheelchair." He adjusted his seat belt, then pointed to the column—mounted levers on the left side of the steering wheel. "Here's my brake, my gas pedal, horn, windshield wipers, and lights—all operable without taking my hands off the steering wheel."

Pride swelled in Megan's heart for the self-reliance Mike demonstrated. She remembered Ken's advice. "Give your young man time to heal, my gal. If he's half the man you say he is, he won't wallow in self-pity for long. My only warning to you is don't mother him; don't try to do everything for him."

While she realized Mike still had a lot of healing to do, the changes since she had left him lying in that hospital bed in Albany were astounding. "I knew you could do it, dear friend," she whispered under her breath. "I knew you'd never settle for less." Out of the corner of her eye, she watched him make the last adjustments. He reminded her of an airline pilot readying for takeoff.

As he reached to put the key in the ignition, their eyes met. He held her gaze. A slow, lazy smile spread across his face. "I could use your help. Would you adjust my coat collar, please? It's twisted in my seat belt."

"Sure thing." She reached across in front of him to straighten the collar when he whispered, "Ya' want a kiss?"

"I'm not falling for that line again."

"Well, you should." He caught her hand in his and lifted it to his lips. "These bucket seats can really cramp one's style," he muttered. He placed his other hand on her back and drew her close.

"I-I thought you meant a Hershey—"

"I know." Mike kissed her lips gently. Tears welled up in her eyes. It had been so long. It was like coming home again.

He released her. His voice grew husky with emotion. "We'd better get home. Mom's expecting us for supper."

Megan nodded and leaned back against her seat.

As he eased the van out into the late afternoon traffic, Mike glanced toward her and grinned. "I wonder if they make two-seater wheelchairs?"

She chuckled and shook her head. "You never quit, do you?"

"Not where you are concerned."

They arrived at the Feldman home as Susan and Kim were setting the dinner table. The family greeted her and drew her into their circle immediately. Throughout the evening she watched Mike as he maneuvered about the house. His agility constantly surprised her. Mike's dad had even adapted the first floor shower stall to make bathing easier for his son. After a long family worship, singing hymns around the piano, everyone went to bed.

The next morning they attended church together. When Megan saw the worshipers in the little sanctuary she immediately relaxed. It was as if she'd been transported back to her home church in New Mexico. Even the soprano who flatted on her high notes during special music seemed like an old friend. On the way home from church, Mike suggested the two of them pack a picnic lunch and go sightseeing.

"That sounds like a great idea. But will your mother mind if we miss dinner with the family?"

He kept his attention on the road ahead. "Naw, I don't think she'll mind at all."

By the time Megan changed into casual clothes and descended to the kitchen, Susan had a large picnic basket stuffed with all sorts of special treats. "Mike prepared most of this yesterday," Susan explained.

"Oh, really?" Megan strolled over to the basket and started to lift one half of the lid when a commanding voice boomed behind her.

"Don't you dare open that any further." Mike rolled into the room. "Patience, my love, patience. But," he gestured dramatically, "if you promise not to look inside, I'll let you carry it out to the van."

She batted her eyelashes, fluttered her hands on her chest and cooed. "I hardly know what to say. You are so kind."

Wil chuckled, "I think you've met your match, son."

"Now Wil," Susan interrupted, "don't go teasing 'em. You kids have a nice day, you hear?"

"You can count on it, Mom," Mike said as he wheeled out the back door and down the ramp. Megan followed with the basket. They climbed into the van.

"Anywhere particular you want to go?" he asked as he started the engine.

"This is your turf, remember?"

They drove north until they found a quiet little spot overlooking Lake George. They parked the van beside an empty picnic table. Once settled at the table, Megan opened the basket. Mike had thought of everything—carrot and celery sticks, three salads, garlic bread, two pieces of carrot cake, and a casserole of homemade lasagna for two—which he informed her he prepared himself—sparkling cider, a blue and white checked tablecloth with matching napkins, a candle melted into an old wine bottle, and matches. Megan placed the food on the table and arranged the table settings.

"Dinner is served," she said with a flourish.

Mike's lower lip protruded into a pout. "You forgot to light the candle."

"In broad daylight?"

"Uh huh."

She shrugged and obeyed. All through their meal the candle glowed in the bright sunlight of the warm May day.

After they had finished and cleaned up the picnic site, Megan and Mike settled back into the van. "Where to now?" Megan asked.

"Lake Champlain and Fort Ticonderoga," Mike said, starting the engine. "Dad gave me a couple of tour tickets to the fort that he got at work."

At the exhibit, guides dressed in full Revolutionary War regalia of the times showed them through the fort. Megan allowed herself to be locked in the courtyard stocks while Mike snapped her picture. She laughed when the guide released her and pointed to the sign overhead "for kissing on Sabbath."

At the end of the tour, Megan and Mike paused beside one of the cannons aimed at the lake. She shaded her eyes from the sun. "The lake is bigger than I imagined."

"Big enough to float a few battleships."

They drove home in silence, a comfortable silence. The day's outing had opened Megan's eyes. Except for an occasional stairstep or curb, Mike managed completely by himself. Much of the time she forgot all about the chair. She was just out enjoying the day with the man she loved.

Once back home, Kim suggested they play Scrabble. While Wil got out the game, Susan microwaved a batch of popcorn.

Megan knew she'd been accepted as a full-fledged member of the clan when she put down the letters "joes" on a triple letter score and Wil challenged it.

"Come on, you can't use a proper noun," he argued.

She grinned and bobbed her head from side to side. "Sorry, joes is plural for jo, a Scottish word meaning sweetheart or dear."

"Hmmph! I don't believe you."

She shrugged. "Look it up."

"Watch out, Dad," Mike warned. "She's shrewd and an English major to boot."

Will grunted as he flipped through the pages of the dictionary. "English major or not . . ." He paused and ran his finger down one column then the next. "Hmmph! So go on Kim, it's your turn."

Susan threw back her head and laughed. "Finally someone in the family who can give you a run for your money, Willy Boy."

Four games and four large bowls of popcorn later, Wil called it quits. "Next time we play, we play teams, it's Megan and me against the rest of you."

"No way!" Kim squealed. "If there are any teams, I'm with Megan all the way."

Megan glanced toward Mike. His eyes glistened with happiness. "Would you like to go for a short walk?" he asked.

She nodded. "I'd love to."

"Better take a sweater, it's cool out there," Susan urged as Mike and Megan headed for the back door.

Wil slipped his arm about his wife's waist and squeezed. "They'll be fine, Mama, just fine."

Megan followed Mike out of the house and strolled down the driveway beside his chair. At the end of the roadway, she paused and looked up. A magnificent array of stars glittered in the navy blue velvet sky. "Oh, it's been so long since I've seen stars so bright. I've missed them, living in the city surrounded by man-made lights." She placed her hand on Mike's arm. "I love lying flat on my back on top of my favorite hill back in New Mexico and searching for constellations. I can't wait to take you there."

"And I can't wait to go. During the last few months, I've thought about all the places you've described, the ranch, your favorite hideaway hill, the mesa overlooking a box canyon, the ghost town, the chapel. I've dreamed of seeing them all one day—with you." He wheeled over to the porch steps. After setting the brake, he lifted himself onto a step. He extended his hand toward her. "Come, sit beside me."

She took his hand and joined him on the step.

He left his hand in hers and leaned back against the porch post. "Your flight leaves early tomorrow morning. But before you leave, we need to have that long talk we promised one another on the phone Thursday night."

Feeling a sharp pain at the thought of leaving, she cupped his hand in hers.

He stared at her profile. "Megan Daniels, I don't think I've ever said this before, but I love you very much."

She turned her head to meet his gaze. His eyes seemed lost in the shadows of the night. "I love you too."

He studied her eyes for some time before he spoke again. "So, where does this leave us? Where do we go from here?"

She scowled. "I don't understand."

"It's all well and good to love one another in the starlight, but the cold reality of morning is something all together different." She started to speak, but he touched her lips with his fingers. "This is not the angry young paraplegic speaking; this is the paraplegic who loves you very much, speaking. You have no idea what you'll be getting into or what you might be giving up if our relationship runs its normal course."

"But I do, at least, in part, I do."

"Are you ready to risk not being able to have children of your own? While the autonomic system that controls my sexual functions was not damaged, I still may not be capable of fathering a child. Are you willing to take that risk?"

Megan thought for a moment. "Is that certain?"

"No, nothing is certain."

"So we're no different than any other unwed couple in that capacity." She started, stopped, then started again. "Mike, I too have had a lot of time to consider us. I've talked to Ken and he told me—"

Mike started. "You talked to a strange man about—"

"Yes," she interrupted, "and he told me that we should consult a therapist when we're ready to consider a permanent relationship. And as far as a family is concerned, of course I'd love to have my own, but let's face it, there are many ways to become parents—look at Mama Grace and her brood."

"Oh, Megan." He cradled both of her hands in his. "I don't want you to one day feel bitter and resentful for what you missed by marrying me."

A mournful moan escaped her lips. "Mike, do you think I'm that shallow? Someone once told me that true love is a meeting of the minds, that it transcends the confines of the human body. Well, for better or worse, my mind has met your mind and frankly, I can't settle for less than the best."

He held her gaze. His voice took on a reflective tone. "But I have no right to deprive you of your dreams and burden you with the rather unpleasant realities of my paralysis."

She turned her face away. "You seem determined to see the limitations. Yes, there are limitations in life—always. I once dreamed of becoming an Olympic gymnast—I'm too old and I'm too tall. Years ago, I also gave up the idea of riding in the Cheyenne rodeo. Life is filled with limitations, but the possibilities far outweigh those foolish barriers, most of which are only found in here." She kissed his forehead. "Don't underestimate me, my love.

"We need to focus on our strengths as a couple. We share the same goals. We like, as well as love each other. We love the same God. We've committed our lives to serving Him. We even both enjoy New York style pizza. What more could we want?"

His chest heaved with laughter as he wrapped his arm about her and pulled her against his shoulder. "You missed your calling. You should have become a lawyer."

She pulled away from him. "I'm not joking. This is serious to me."

He sobered instantly. "And to me."

"So, as you asked earlier, what happens next?"

He cleared his throat. "I think you need to go back to New York and finish out the school term, and I need to stay here and continue with my therapy."

She tapped out her impatience on the sidewalk with the toe of her sneaker. "Then what?"

He reached across and drew lazy circles on her shoulder. "Well, you need to carry out your plans for graduate school."

"What? Spend the summer at the university in Michigan with you here in Glens Falls? That will really help our love to grow."

Mike heaved a heavy sigh. "I have two worries, Megan, that I must exorcise before we make a formal commitment. My first is for you to date other men."

"But-but-but—" she sputtered.

He threw up his hands in front of his face. "Hey, I'm not underestimating you in the slightest. I just need to be certain that you are certain and that we've given God time."

"And the second worry?"

"I need to prove to myself I can live independently—that I can survive on my own. I don't want to go straight from my mother's care to my wife's care. I need to feel that I am a man, not an animated vegetable."

She stared out into the darkness. "How are you going to do this?"

"I plan to get my own apartment down near the hospital. The chaplain wants me to put in more hours with the kids. I'm beginning to think I've found my calling, at least for the time being." His eyes sparkled with enthusiasm. He caressed the side of her cheek. "Eleven months, is that so long?"

Her throat tightened. The little laugh she forced bore no resemblance to the sound of mirth. "I'll do it, but I won't like it."

He ran his fingers through her long tangle of curls. "I'll write everyday and call you every week and I'll send the money to pay for your airfare whenever you can break away from school." He lifted her hair and placed a long, warm kiss on the nape of her neck.

"Don't," she whispered and arched her neck away from him.

Mike sat back and closed his eyes. Megan's mind fought against the wisdom of his request. She felt a tightening in her chest that was half protest and half dreadful understanding. The lightness of her tone was strained, her voice unsteady. "Eleven months and then we have a summit meeting to renegotiate the terms?"

His hand came up to touch her chin lightly, turning her face upward to him; his eyes begged for understanding. "Eleven months, that's all. And you will promise to date other men, won't you?"

She groaned aloud. "That's easier said than done. I can't just walk up to a strange man and ask him for a date."

Something softened in his voice. "Just promise, OK?"

"Do you want me to give you a full report of every date?"

"No, that won't be necessary. But I do want you to remember this." His hand cupped gently around her neck. Warm, strong fingers drew her to him. He leaned forward and kissed her. It was a gentle, loving, reassuring kiss that spoke of promises for the future—their future.

15

Megan threw her loaded suitcase on the bed. *Future! Future! What kind of future can we possibly have with him a thousand miles away and me all alone in the cornfields of Michigan?* she protested to herself. That there were no cornfields in sight didn't deter her from venting her frustration. *Mike and his bright ideas!*

Though Michigan State offered some surprises, she was soon back into the student routine again. After being a teacher for so long, it was a welcome relief. After the usual confusion of summer registration and orientation, Megan charged into her studies. Each morning she took notes at lectures. Each afternoon she deciphered her notes. Evenings she studied in the library. And each night she fell into bed exhausted. Her only pleasure was the letter waiting for her in her dorm mailbox at the end of each day. On Friday night, she looked forward to an extra-long hot shower and to her two phone calls—one from her father at 9:15 and one from Mike at 9:30.

Her dad and Libby's happiness seemed to radiate over the phone, setting the tone for Mike's call. After the first few weeks of talking until midnight, she and Mike decided they needed to set a time limit when they talked or they'd soon go broke. His enthusiasm about his work at the hospital and his ability to function on his own spilled into the conversation every time they talked. He never asked if she'd dated anyone that week, but she could tell he ached to. *Well, let him wonder,* she thought.

Megan had a study-date or two with a single high school history teacher who was there only for the summer session. They'd studied *Adolescent Psychology* over a couple cans of diet 7-Up. A guy from her *Curriculum* class carried her stack of library books back to the dorm for her one evening. But in general, the summer session was relatively quiet. Then came the regular term and 3,000 eager students.

During freshman orientation week, she flew to Albany to spend two days with Mike. She arranged to stay with Mama Grace's sister once again. Mike had told her about a therapist he'd been seeing at a clinic called, "Adaptability Unlimited."

"I don't know what I would do without Dr. Cruthers," Mike admitted. "He has made all the difference in the world. He's shown me how to live a full and independent life. My biggest fear after I accepted the fact I was paralyzed, was that I might spend the rest of my life a burden to those I love." He stared down at his hands. "I couldn't stand to do that to you—make you a slave to my bodily functions."

With her permission, Mike arranged for them to talk with the therapist together. Megan liked the psychologist immediately. Dr. Cruthers helped them admit to each other their feelings and expectations. He suggested that when she returned to Michigan, Megan should look up a support group for spouses near the university.

"The group will be able to answer questions you don't even know you have yet. For instance, the medical reports indicate that Mike's ability to father children is no more or no less than any other young man his age. However, there are other issues you probably haven't considered."

Megan looked the doctor straight in the eye. "That, sir, is not an option."

"You think not now, but you can't be certain until you face the very real upheaval such injuries cause." She watched the doctor scribble a name on the back of his business card. "Here is the name of a colleague of mine—Dr. Judith Barber who lives near the university you're attending. She specializes in family and sexual problems of the physically impaired. She's easy to talk to and a wealth of information."

On Sunday, Megan reluctantly kissed Mike goodbye at the airport and flew back to Michigan.

Between her world of assignments and term papers, and meeting two nights a week with the support group, the weeks sped by for Megan. She enjoyed her occasional visits with Dr. Barber. Talking with the tiny, fiftyish, sprite of a woman proved to be a highlight in her routine. The psychologist's straight forward, yet upbeat attitude helped Megan see possibilities instead of problems, hope as well as reality.

At the support group meetings, Megan liked the change of pace, interacting with a variety of people not controlled by grade point averages and late night study sessions. Most of the group were spouses learning how to cope with varying forms of disability. A couple of the group were adult children whose parents had been injured in accidents. One man was the brother of a plane crash victim. A quadriplegic man about the age of Ken led the discussion.

For a few hours, Megan could escape her books, relax and ask questions without pressure. Sometimes she blushed at the direct way her questons were answered. She'd never discussed such topics so openly with anyone but her dad. And maybe not even with him, she realized.

One Thursday night after a late study session, Megan's two worlds collided. Loaded to her eyebrows with library books, she stepped off the curb just as a battered VW bug rounded the corner. She bounced off the front fender onto the grassy island between the road and the sidewalk; her books flew in every direction.

The driver hopped out of his car and ran to her side. "Oh, I'm so sorry. Are you OK? Should I call an ambulance?"

She patted her arms and her legs, then groaned. "My favorite stockings are ruined," she wailed. "Otherwise, I guess I'm still in one piece."

With little effort the tall muscular man lifted her to her feet. She staggered. "Can you stand all right or should I carry you? Honest, I didn't see you in the dark."

"I should have looked more carefully before I stepped off the curb. I'm afraid my mind was elsewhere." The evening breeze caused a sheet of notebook paper to flutter by. "My books! My term paper!" She glanced frantically about the paper strewn area.

"Here, you sit while I collect your stuff." He helped her to the car and opened the door. The overhead light popped on illuminating Megan's face.

"Don't I know you?"

She'd intended to tell him how trite his come-on was, but bit back her words when he leaned down into the pool of light. "Hey, you're the guy in the support group. Your brother was injured in a plane crash, right?"

He knelt down beside the open car door. "Right. I thought I recognized you. You're the one who's boyfriend sent her away to school, huh? You attend the university?"

"Yes, I'm a graduate student."

"Me too. I'm Sean Conners, a third year law student." His blond curly hair flopped down on his forehead. "Hey, let me gather your stuff together. I'd like to take you over to the all night cafe for a cup of hot chocolate or something to settle your nerves."

Before Megan realized what had happened, she found herself sitting opposite a stranger who really wasn't a stranger at all. Sean had just finished telling about his on-going battle with his hard-rock loving roommate when a frightening thought shook her self-confidence. *I'm enjoying myself. I can't enjoy myself with Sean. I love Mike.*

She rubbed her arms to ward off a sudden chill. "I've got to get back to the dorm. I-I'll see you around, Sean. Thanks for the hot chocolate."

He leaped to his feet and helped her from the booth. "Let me drive you back to the dorm, it's the least I can do after trying to run you down with my car." Dimples appeared at the corners of his mouth. Dimples almost as cute as Mike's. She paled at the thought.

"No!" She grabbed her books in her arms and bolted toward the exit. "I'd rather walk. Thank you anyway."

She hurried back to the dormitory and into her room. After slipping into a nightgown and robe, Megan tiptoed down to one of the prayer rooms on her floor. She spent the night on her knees, trying to make sense out of her jumbled thoughts.

The next morning Megan skipped her literature class to go and see the school chaplain. She told him about Mike and the agreement they'd made, and about what had happened the night before.

"I love Mike with all my heart," she said. "He's everything I want in a husband. Besides having the same values and beliefs as I do, he's witty, intelligent, sensitive, strong, and wise—did I say sensitive? The list goes on and on."

"I see." The gray-haired chaplain leaned back in his desk chair and urged her to continue.

"But if I love Mike so much, then why was I attracted to Sean? What if this happens after we've been married for five or ten years?" She ran her fingers through her hair. "I'm scared. Maybe I don't know myself after all. I mean, when it comes to men, I've been wrong before."

The chaplain leaned forward, his hands folded on the desktop in front of him. "Do you think that once you fall in love you will never be attracted to a handsome man again? That you will no longer enjoy talking with a member of the opposite sex? Love is more than attraction."

Megan remembered her conversation with Mike on his front porch.

"Love is a meeting of the minds," she whispered.

"That's right," the chaplain answered. "This may come as a surprise to you, but throughout your marriage you will meet individuals to whom you are attracted. That's why you sign a contract where you vow to 'forsake all others and keep only unto him as long as ye both shall live.' Marriage goes beyond the emotional roller coaster of courtship, it's a mind-set—a conscious, well-thought-out choice."

"I guess I have a lot to think and pray about this weekend, huh?" Megan rose to her feet.

The chaplain circled the desk to her side and took her hand in his. "May I give you one piece of advice? Be very sure of your feelings before you turn your back on this Mike person. He sounds like a wise young man."

She nodded enthusiastically. "Oh, he is. He really is."

Skipping the rest of her classes, Megan took her Bible and walked to the city park. She seated herself on a bench beside a duck pond for an afternoon of Bible study and prayer.

She watched the sunlight sparkling on the surface of the water. The memory of a camping trip in Colorado one summer with her parents came to mind. She was playing in a stream next to their camp-site when she found gold flecks scattered along the bank. She ran back to the tent to tell her dad how rich they were going to be. He had chuckled.

"That's pyrite, Megan," he had said kindly. "Folks call it 'fool's gold.' A lot of people have been fooled just like you have; some have lost their lives in their pursuit of something practically worthless." Herb had looked at her seriously. "Don't ever be fooled with the imitation. Pyrite isn't gold."

She had no doubt that Michael Feldman was the genuine article— solid gold through and through. She'd be foolish to risk losing the real thing for unknown quality, no matter how bright it may shine in the sunlight. By the time Mike called that evening, Megan's doubts had dissolved. She knew her mind and her heart. Eleven months, eleven years—it really didn't matter. He was worth the wait.

Since she'd be flying home to New Mexico for Christmas, Megan chose to stay on campus for the short Thanksgiving break. Mike called on Thanksgiving day. They talked longer than usual. He described his furnished efficiency apartment, down to the pots and pans he bought at the Goodwill store. She told him about the study-dates she'd gone on, as well as the occasional Saturday night lyceums she'd attended with various individuals. And she told him about Sean.

"Will you be seeing this Sean fellow again?" he asked. Megan could tell by Mike's slow, controlled reply that he'd sensed the difference between her casual encounters with fellow graduate students and the evening with Sean.

Her first instinct was to scream at him. "No! Haven't you been listening to what I've been saying?" Instead, she adopted a cool, nonchalant tone. "Who knows? Do you think I should?"

"Well, I suppose, if you think you want to."

She plopped herself down in the middle of her bed. "Oh, Michael, it's not what I want, it's what you've been bugging me to do. Sometimes, it's as if . . . oh, I don't know. Trying to maintain a long distance relationship is for the birds!"

"I know," he said. "I know."

After Megan hung up from their conversation, she felt so alone. *Will Mike ever believe me—that I look at him with love, not pity?* she wondered. She gave his limitations as much thought as she gave her own—such as wearing contact lenses all the time. Why couldn't he see himself in a similar way?

Having no pressures over the Thanksgiving holiday weekend, Megan relaxed. She hitched a ride with a group of stranded students to the mall and did some Christmas shopping. She found a watch she knew Mike would enjoy, but resisted the urge since he might misunderstand her intent. She bought him an engraved pen and pencil set instead. After buying gifts for his family and for Mama Grace, the children, and Sara, she mailed them off.

The next two weeks of late night studying, typing final drafts on term papers, and taking exams flew by in record time. Almost before she realized it, she found herself aboard a plane and heading home to New Mexico for the holidays.

Her dad talked non-stop from the moment she stepped off the plane until they pulled into the long drive leading to the ranch. "It's just going to be the greatest Christmas in years, kiddo. Libby has been baking for weeks now, ever since she washed the last of Thanskgiving Day's pots and pans, I think. And the tree, wait until you see the tr—" Suddenly he stopped talking and glanced toward his daughter. His eyes filled with happiness. "Oh, Meggy, I've missed you so much."

She buried her face in his shoulder. "I missed you too, Daddy."

On Christmas eve, the three of them climbed into the truck and drove to Albuquerque's Old Town. There, along with hundreds of others, they gathered in the town square to sing Christmas carols. Luminarias—simple brown lunch bags, partially filled with sand and illuminated with a candle set inside, lined the walkways. Megan's eyes danced like a child's.

"I didn't realize how much I missed this last year," she bubbled. "Mike would just love this." After the celebration in town, Libby suggested they drive through the residential neighborhoods to see the homes and yards also decorated with the luminarias.

On Christmas morning, after all the other gifts under the tree had been opened, Libby dragged out a large box from the den. "This arrived for you last week, but I had already been instructed by phone not to let you see it until today. Mrs. Feldman gave strict orders."

Megan tore open the carton. Inside were a number of brightly wrapped packages. She read the tags on each one. "Daddy, this is for you from the Feldmans. Here's one for you Libby. And one, two, three for me."

Her father and Libby received matching navy and white woolen ski sweaters made in Canada. Megan's first package contained a matching hand-made red woolen scarf and ski cap from Wil and Susan Feldman. "This is what I worked on during the long days of Mike's convalescence," Susan explained in the attached note. Kim sent a bottle of cologne. The third package contained a large tin of homemade candy for the entire family. Megan took a piece and passed the container to Libby, then on to Herb.

"My weakness," he groaned as he savored his first bite.

Libby rose to her feet and scooped up a handful of discarded wrapping paper and bows. "Ready for a traditional Christmas breakfast of Bavarian waffles?"

The first waffles had just come off the grill when the telephone rang. Megan leaped to her feet. "I'll get it."

"Reminds me of when you were 13 or 14," her father called as she disappeared from the room.

She ran into her father's den and picked up the receiver. "Daniel's res—hi, Mike, Merry Christmas." She dropped into her father's upholstered reclining chair and put her feet up on his desk.

"Merry Christmas to you, too, sweetheart."

Each of the family wanted to say hi and wished her a Merry Christmas. They thanked her for their gifts and returned the phone to Mike. "Thank you for the pen set," he said. "Your gift from me will be waiting for you back at school."

She leaned further back in the chair. "So, are you going to give me any hints or are you going to torture me?"

"Torture! Definitely torture! By the way, what's your flight schedule?"

"I leave here New Year's Day at 5:00 p.m. I have an hour and a half layover at O'Hare. Then I take a puddle jumper across the lake to Benton Harbor. I should get in sometime before midnight, I suppose." She rotated the desk chair back and forth as she talked.

"What airline are you flying?"

"TWA, flight 1007. Why?"

"Just curious. You will call and tell me you landed safely, won't you?"

She rocked back and forth in the chair. "Sure, if you want me to."

"Of course I want you to."

She jumped up from the chair and prepared to hang up. "OK, will do." They ended their conversation soon after.

The night before she was to leave for school, Libby begged off from hiking up to Megan's favorite overlook with Megan and her dad. Megan stared at the stars that punctuated the black winter sky. "I really do love him, Dad. I don't want to lose him."

Her father chuckled. "That's news? All you've talked about since you got home was Mike and how much he'd enjoy whatever we did or wherever we went."

She placed her hand on his arm. "I'm sorry. I didn't mean —"

"Honey, that's OK. Libby and I understand."

Megan kicked at a pebble, sending it cascading to the bottom of the canyon. "He can't seem to get past the physical problems we might encounter in our marriage. Sometimes I think it's all his male ego or something."

"It might have been in the beginning, but I don't think it is now. He loves you, kiddo. Give him time."

"Daddy," she began, running her hand along his stubbled chin, "have I ever said thank you for being the kind of dad a kid can respect. Whenever I think of God's love and His faithfulness, I think of you." Her father cleared his throat and squeezed her hand tightly. Arm in arm, they made their way back to the house.

The next day, her father and Libby drove her to the airport. When her flight was called for loading, the three of them drew together in a circle and prayed. She kissed her father's moist cheek and he kissed hers. Both sensed that Megan's departure this time was different from the many times she'd left home before.

Thanks to a stack of magazines supplied by the airline and to her seat partner, a teenage girl experiencing her first plane ride, the three hour flight passed quickly. Due to the holiday traffic, planes were stacked up over O'Hare. Finally her plane touched down and taxied to the terminal. Knowing she had at least an hour and a half before boarding her next flight, she waited for the plane to empty, then fell in behind the last stragglers.

She stepped out of the flight corridor into a waiting area filled with strangers, all of which were applauding her. "What in the w—" She gaped in surprise. Clusters of multicolored balloons floated above the heads of the crowd. Taped to the ends of the balloon's ribbons were chocolate kisses and notes reading, "Let me shower you with kisses." A long trail of computer paper stretched across the archway between the waiting area and the main causeway. In bold, primary colors, it read, "I love you, Megan Daniels. Will you marry me?"

The color drained from her face, then she blushed bright red. She scanned the sea of smiling strangers for a familiar face. "Mike?"

"Right here." He sat off to one side in his chair. He held three dozen long-stemmed red roses on his lap. The onlookers grew silent as she turned in the direction of his voice.

She dropped her carry-on case and stared. "Mike! What are you doing here?"

"I thought that was obvious. I'm asking you to marry me. So will you?"

A man from the crowd yelled out. "Yeah, lady, will you?"

"Wait," Mike held up a free hand and the crowd grew silent again. "Let's do this right." He maneuvered the chair to her side and placed the flowers in her arms. He stared into her bewildered eyes. For a moment, they were alone in a world made only for two. "Megan, I do love you with all my heart. Will you be my wife, my friend, and my lover for life?"

She opened her mouth to reply but no words came out. She nodded. A thunderous cheer went up from the enthusiastic crowd. Clutching the bouquet of roses to her chest, she knelt beside his chair and kissed him. He wrapped his arms about her and buried his face in her shoulder. The people cheered again.

How long they held each other, they didn't know. When they looked up, most of the crowd had dispersed toward their own destinations.

Megan wiped the tears from her cheeks and stood up.

"We'd better get going. We have a two-hour drive to Michigan," Mike reminded. "We'll have to pick up your luggage in Benton Harbor tomorrow."

"Whatever made you do all of this?" she asked. "I've never been so stunned."

"Sean What's-his-name."

Megan placed the roses in Mike's lap and retrieved her purse and carry-on case. "You were jealous?"

"No—er, yeah, I guess I was," he admitted. "But it was more than that. There was a difference in the way you talked about him. Suddenly I knew I didn't want to lose you." He paused. "When I told my dad about Sean and our arrangement, he said, 'Don't push this nobility thing too far, Mike. Remember, a faint heart never won a fair lady.' "

Megan laughed. "He said that?"

"Once I decided to drive out here to meet you and to ask you to marry me, the entire family just about pushed me out the door." He threw his hands up in amazement. "I managed to convince them to let me stay at least until the day after Christmas."

While Mike began gathering up loose balloons, Megan took the sign down and folded it carefully. "Someday, I want to show this to our children. I still can't believe it. You must have been pretty sure of yourself to pull off such an extravaganza."

"Not really. It's just that I'd balked so often and voiced so many doubts along the way, I had to be certain that you knew that all of my fears regarding us had been laid to rest."

"Well, you succeeded," she admitted, shifting her bundle of balloons to her other hand. "Just how many of these things did you buy?"

Mike laughed. "Oh, 50 or so—give or take a few."

"You drove to the airport with 50 balloons bobbing around your head in the van?"

"No, I got them here at one of the shops," he explained. "The manager gave me a special price since I was buying so many. One of the clerks in the shop helped me tape the candies to the ribbons and helped me carry them to the waiting area. Once I got here and explained my intent to the ticket agent, I had more than enough help putting up the sign and arranging the balloons."

She shook her head in disbelief. "You are a nut case! A real nut case!"

They joined the other travelers and made their way down the causeway, giving away balloons to the children they met. Once Mike and Megan reached the privacy of his van, he extracted a black velvet case from the glove compartment and opened it. Her breath caught in her throat as he fastened a delicate gold watch onto her wrist, then placed a kiss on her lips. "Merry Christmas, my love." He softly caressed her cheek, then straightened. "By the way, your father sends his love. I called him today."

"You what? Why?"

"You are so precious to me that I don't want to risk losing you. Therefore, I decided to observe all the rules governing a Christian courtship—including the age-old custom of asking for your hand in marriage." He buckled his seat belt and inserted the key in the ignition. The engine roared to life. "It will be worth it in the long run to do everything God's way. Oh, I have another surprise I hope you'll like."

She eyed him nervously. "Let me guess. You arranged to have the university band playing 'I Love You Truly' on the women's dormitory lawn when we get back to campus, right?"

He shook with laughter. "I would have if I'd thought of it."

She groaned. "Somehow I believe you. So what's your latest surprise?"

He backed the van out of the parking spot. "I applied to a graduate school in Indiana—just ten miles from you. I explained my situation and they almost guaranteed me over the telephone that I'd be accepted. I'll know by Thursday."

"That's wonderful!" she squealed with delight. "I don't believe it. I don't know what to say."

As he pulled onto the highway, he told her he had decided to pursue a master's degree in counseling. The financial arrangements he'd been able to make with various government agencies guaranteed his tuition. "Later, maybe I'll finish my theology degree. Right now, there are kids who have been injured in motorcycle accidents or suffering from other tragedies. They need to know their lives aren't over."

Mile after mile they drove through the darkness. Megan bubbled with happiness as Mike shared his dreams. He had changed so much. And she liked the changes. This wasn't the bitter young man who'd sent her from his side, nor was it the old Mike with whom she'd toured the city of New York. This Mike had a maturity, a confidence, and a focus the others' lacked. She recognized in him an inner peace, the kind of peace that remains after winning a victory over pain. Yes, indeed, Michael Feldman had become a triumphant survivor, just like Ken had promised. And even more importantly, just like God had promised.

CHAPTER

16

Garlands of blue satin ribbon, Queen Anne's lace, and field daisies scalloped across the rostrum of the once abandoned chapel. Megan slid her hands into her jean pockets and shook her head at her sister-to-be. "The right strand needs to come up a bit, Kim."

"Gotcha." The young girl made the adjustment. "Is that better?"

Behind her, Sara stood talking with Libby and Susan about the parents' processional, Vivaldi's "Ode to Spring." Megan laughed to herself. When Sara discovered she would have to play the wedding march on Granny Caldwell's nineteenth-century pump organ, she was terrified.

"I have a hard enough time getting it right without remembering to pump the crazy thing," she had exclaimed. But Granny Caldwell would have none of it.

"My stubborn old German grandmother hauled that organ over the Oregon Trail in 1866 — all the way from Boston" the 85-year-old woman said. "My grandpa Herman blustered up a storm, but Grandma Jenny insisted. Now after all that work I don't see how you can complain about having to pump a little. Besides" — Granny Caldwell beamed with pride — "it's traditional."

Megan scanned the chapel once more before leaving to dress for the ceremony. *It couldn't be more perfect,* she thought. *How many people get to see a childhood fantasy come to life?*

It all started when Mike talked to her father about holding the wedding in the abandoned chapel at Cerrillos. "Is it at all possible?" Mike asked.

"Well, I don't rightly know, but I'll find out. I suppose we'd have to get permission from the state historical society."

The state authorities jumped at the chance to have the old church restored. When Pastor Hinkley and the members of her father's church learned of the project, they got involved. After two Sunday morning work sessions, they'd whitewashed the smoke-stained walls and scrubbed the floors until they shone. Other families still living around the town saw what the strangers were doing and joined in the cleanup. By the weekend of the ceremony, everything right down to the rough hewn oak benches glistened with fresh paint and varnish.

Other surprises were in store. A photojournalist from a national brides' magazine heard of the renovation and contacted Megan's father. He wanted to cover the wedding for his editors and in exchange, he'd make them up a full set of wedding pictures. Friends from all over the United States drove through or flew in to join in the celebration.

The day before the ceremony, the local church members, as well as the residents of the town, held a special worship service together in the chapel. Pastor Hinkley reminded everyone that we need not fear the future as long as we remember how God has led in the past. After the service, Megan and Mike stood at the door with the pastor and invited each person to the next day's celebration.

And now on Sunday morning, her wedding day, Megan surveyed the interior of desert chapel once more. From the youngest child to the oldest saint, from Ph.Ds to society drop-outs, from inner-city residents to cattle ranchers, all had worked together to create the miracle. *Mom would have loved this,* Megan thought as she ran her hand along the back of the nearest pew.

"Megan!" Sara tapped her on the shoulder. "You need to go and take a long bubble bath or something. We've got everything under control here."

"Kim, where's Kim?" Megan asked. "She asked to ride back to the ranch with me."

"She's waiting for you in the truck."

Megan followed Sara out of the chapel and down the temporary ramp her father had constructed. Off to one side, under a grove of eucalyptus trees, Mama Grace and a group of ladies were setting up the buffet tables for the reception. Ken sat in his wheelchair at the far end of the tables, folding paper napkins. When he spied Megan coming out of the church, his face broke into a neon smile. "Go home!" he shouted, waving her toward the parking area. "Go home!"

"Yes, sir!" She saluted as she walked past. "I'm on my way." She drove at record speed over the rutted dirt road, back to the paved county road and home. Kim leaped from the cab of the truck almost before it came to a stop and disappeared into the house. By the time Megan climbed out of the cab and entered the empty kitchen, Kim was nowhere in sight. Megan walked into the parlor. She idly ran her fingers across the keys of the old upright piano and glanced at her mother's photograph. She had been pleased to discover that instead of removing Megan's mother's photo from the piano, Libby had added those of her family, including one of her first husband.

"Hi, honey." Her father, decked out in his best suit, strode across the carpet to where Megan stood. He placed his arm around her waist and drew her close. "I imagine you'll see your wedding picture lined up here with all the rest." She smiled and rested the back of her head against his shoulder. "You've become quite a woman, Meggy darlin', since your journey to New York City. Seemed like a terrible idea at the time. As usual, God knew better than I just what you really needed."

The grandfather clock beside the fireplace struck 11:00. Startled, Megan kissed her father on the cheek. "I'd better get going or there won't be any wedding," she called as she bounded up the stairs to her room. She grabbed her robe and raced for the shower. *Bubble bath indeed*, she mused as the cool spray pelted her face. *Who has time for a bubble bath today of all days?*

From the moment she stepped out of the shower, her life shifted into automatic. Not taking the time to do more than blow dry her hair, she and Kim drove back to Cerrillos. She stepped from the truck into a frenzy of antique lace, hairspray, laughter, and tears.

"Quick," Sara squealed, "let's do something with that hair of yours." She led Megan to a small table and chair in front of a wall mirror. "Sit!" With a comb in one hand and a can of hairspray in the other, Sara began styling Megan's hair.

She grimaced at her reflection as Sara began spraying generous amounts of hair spray at Megan's long tresses. "Remember, I don't want it too stiff."

"I know, I know." Sara continued combing and spraying.

Megan closed her eyes and wailed, "I can't look. I just can't look."

Sara laughed and squirted another layer of lacquer on Megan's growing mountain of hair. "Relax, trust me."

"Right," Megan coughed from the spray. "Isn't that what Custer said at Little Big Horn?"

Kim tapped her on her shoulder. "How do I look?" Megan opened her eyes. The excited maid of honor whirled about in her blue-and-white organdy and gingham gown. A blue satin bow matching the one around her waist held her hair in a cluster of dark cascading curls down the back of her head.

"You look beautiful, Kim."

The young girl giggled and tossed her curls from side to side. "I feel like Mary on 'Little House on the Prairie.'"

Megan shook with laughter.

"Hold still," Sara wailed. "This curling iron is hot. There, you can move now. That was the last of the tendrils." She sprayed Megan's hair once more, then stepped back to take a look. "Just like we practiced. Now, let's get you into that gown. It's going to take forever buttoning all of those tiny satin buttons!"

They watched Libby slip the white organdy wedding gown from its protective plastic bag. Megan removed her cotton robe and lifted her arms to allow Libby and Susan to guide the antique wedding dress down over her head. She gently guided her arms into the fingertip lace sleeves and waited as the two women buttoned the dress.

"You were right about the dress, dear friend," Sara whispered as she twisted one of the long wispy curls around Megan's face into place. Sara fastened the wreath of daisies, English tea roses, satin ribbons, and veiling atop Megan's Gibson girl hairdo and lowered the whisper-fine veil down over her face. "It suits you perfectly."

Megan never doubted it would from the moment she'd spotted the wedding dress in a vintage clothing store in Benton Harbor. Yet she felt like a little girl playing dress up.

"But now I have to get over to the chapel and pump some music out of that old hurdy-gurdy." Sara hurried from the room, but Megan hardly noticed. She stared at the stranger reflected in the full length mirror, a woman from a different era. *It's like I'm living in the middle of an old time western*, Megan thought as she studied her reflection. *But it's not an old time western. It's today and it's me.*

A knot of panic tightened in her stomach, then surfaced in the eyes of the woman looking back at her. "Can I do this?" she whispered to herself. But no one heard. Instead, someone shoved a bouquet of flowers in her hands and led her from the building. Somewhere in the distance she could hear Sara playing the old pump organ. The hot June sun dazzled her eyes as she crossed the courtyard to the chapel. Her attendants spoke to her, but she had no idea what they were saying. She felt, rather than saw, her father take her hand, and place it in his arm, then lead her up the ramp into the church foyer.

I can't cry now, she thought. *I can't cry now.* She could hear the wedding coordinator lining up the attendants for the processional. She heard someone say, "The place is packed. There are people standing along the walls."

As the doors swung open and the first bridesmaid started down the aisle, Megan turned to her father, her gray eyes filled with terror. "Daddy," she whispered, "I don't think I can do this."

Her father glanced down at her and frowned for a moment, then smiled. "Do you know that your mother uttered the very same words to your grandfather in the car on the way to our wedding?"

Her lower lip trembled. "Really? I never knew that." When the majestic chords of Mendelssohn's Wedding March filled the air, the audience rose to their feet.

"Psst! It's your turn," the coordinator urged.

As they took their first step forward, her father whispered, "Forget everyone else and just keep your eyes on Mike."

Slowly Megan turned her face toward the scared young man waiting for her at the end of the aisle. When their eyes met, his tight nervous smile widened into a joyous grin. His eyes sparkled with tears of happiness. She could feel his love reaching out to her, drawing her. Her fears melted as she glided to his side. Megan's father kissed her goodbye and lifted her hand from his arm and placed it in Mike's outstretched hand.

She felt the familiar warmth and strength of Mike's hand as he led her to the altar. While Sara's clear soprano voice carried a message about cherishing one another, Megan gazed into Mike's tear-filled eyes. Silently, he mouthed the words, "Never will I leave you; never will I forsake you."

The first time he'd quoted those words to her they were standing on the observation deck of the Empire State Building. How different the circumstances were then. So much had happened; so much had changed. Through the good times as well as the bad, she had claimed that promise so often since. And now, here, standing at the altar, about to promise her love and her faithfulness to this man, he gave the words an entirely new meaning.

"Never will I leave you; never will I forsake you," a wedding vow pledged between a perfect God, a man and a woman; a promise that would bind two hearts to one another for life, and to God for all eternity.

Also by Kay Rizzo

Gospel in the Grocery Store
These lighthearted parables spring from trips to the
supermarket—the unruly shopping cart, the impersonal mob, a
loaf of wheat bread, and generic products in their insignificant
wrappers—and reveal eye-opening truths about ourselves, God,
and the people in our lives. Paper, 95 pages. US$4.95, Cdn$6.20.

Someone to Love Me
A daughter lives in a secret misery created by her stepmother
and pistol-waving father. This is the story of how she found love
and a Saviour. Paper, 94 pages. US$6.95, Cdn$8.70.

Up Against the Wall
An Italian immigrant finds himself wandering the dirty streets of
a New York City ghetto determined to survive in spite of
disaster, hunger, prejudice, and hate. He's up against a wall, but
a compassionate woman and a caring God will change his life
forever. Paper, 96 pages. US$6.95, Cdn$8.70.

To order, call **1-800-765-6955** or write to ABC Mailing Service, P.O. Box
1119, Hagerstown, MD 21741. Send check or money order. Enclose
applicable sales tax and 15 percent (minimum US$2.50) for postage and
handling. Prices and availability subject to change without notice. Add 7
percent GST in Canada.

Inspiring Stories
of God's Healing Grace

Because of Patty
When a phantom illness struck Sam and Mella's infant daughter, it should have been a tragedy. But their night of despair turned to joy because of Patty. This is a heartwarming story filled with a mother and father's anguish and dreams, sleepless nights, and tender moments with a little girl who always gave more than she took. By Paula Montgomery. Paper, 126 pages. US$7.95, Cdn$9.95.

The Heart and Soul of Landon Harris
It had all been a mistake, Landon thought. Leaving Joetta, marrying power-hungry Diana, then divorcing her. All that mattered now were his son and stepson, and that he might lose them. He desperately wanted to start over, and God was his only hope. A compelling story about a single father's quest for God and new beginnings with his family. By Helen Godfrey Pyke. Paper, 140 pages. US$7.95, Cdn$9.95.

Love's Bitter Victory
How do you tell your child you're sorry for missing the first 24 years of his life? Laura Michaels begins a journey away from alcoholism and discovers Jesus, a new start with her son, and a joy so contagious that it begins to change the broken lives around her. By Midge Nayler. Paper, 187 pages. US$8.95, Cdn$11.20.

To order, call **1-800-765-6955** or write to ABC Mailing Service, P.O. Box 1119, Hagerstown, MD 21741. Send check or money order. Enclose applicable sales tax and 15 percent (minimum US$2.50) for postage and handling. Prices and availability subject to change without notice. Add 7 percent GST in Canada.